Out of the Comfort Zone

Out of the Comfort Zone

From the Appalachians to the Atlantic Ocean

Kenneth A. Luikart

Xulon Press

Xulon Press
2301 Lucien Way #415
Maitland, FL 32751
407.339.4217
www.xulonpress.com

xulon PRESS

Completed June 20, 2020

Printed in the United States of America.

Paperback ISBN-13: 978-1-6322-1546-8
eBook ISBN-13: 978-1-6322-1547-5

This book is dedicated to my wife, Sandi, whose help and guidance produced a great little book!

Table of Contents

Preface

My third book in *The Comfort Zone* series is dedicated to my wife, Sandra Lynn (Sandi) Bardell. She's the girl that I fell in love with instantly, then married, and to this day, she is still my wife. Sandi is my chief editor, as well as the financier of my books. This book is also dedicated to my son and his wife, Jamey and Amanda Luikart, and to my daughter and her husband, Jennifer and Matt Russell.

But more importantly, this book is dedicated to my three grandsons Roman Russell, Alexander Russell, and Nathan Luikart. They are the "three little hills that skipped around like lambs (Ps. 114: 4)." They are the main reasons I have penned this series about my life.

There may be other books in my future if time will allow. I'm in my seventies, and I'm blind in one eye. However, this book will open the reader to my trip to Florida for love and for all the right reasons. Sandi kept me alive during my bouts with Post Traumatic Stress Disorder (PTSD) and anger issues. She is the glue that binds our family.

I hope all enjoy my books. I am thinking of writing a few more books in this series. Time will tell. God Bless you all.

Statement of Faith

1 When Israel went out of Egypt, the house of Jacob
from a people of strange language; **2** Judah was his
sanctuary, *and* Israel his dominion. **3** The sea saw
it, and fled: Jordan was driven back.

4 The mountains skipped like rams, *and* the little
hills like lambs. **5** What *ailed* thee, O thou sea, that
thou fleddest? thou Jordan, *that* thou wast driven
back? **6** Ye mountains, *that* ye skipped like rams;
and ye little hills, like lambs?

7 Tremble, thou earth, at the presence of the Lord,
at the presence of the God of Jacob; **8** Which turned
the rock *into* a standing water, the flint into a fountain of waters.

Psalm 114, KJV

Chapter 1

The Letters–1970

Sitting out back of the house, late one afternoon in the shade of an umbrella, I was contentedly watching water from our pond spilling from the first level to the second, and then to the third. The cascading rivulets of water created a soothing sound. I had just come outside from re-reading and bundling up letters that Sandi had sent me when I was stationed in Baltimore in 1970. Now five decades old, those letters are as sweet and relevant today as they were then.

I had also been leafing through fourteen work-diary books that I had kept while working for Union Camp Forest Research. Most of my adult life was spent working in the silviculture industry as a forest technician, or forest ranger. I wanted to make sure that the most important parts of those work diaries, as well as Sandi's letters, survived for my grandkids and their kids.

My reflections caused me to realize that I also wanted to tell Boy Scout stories, and at that point I knew I had a book that needed writing. I'm in my 43rd year of Scouting and will soon be 73 years old. I was a young man when I started in scouting; where did the days go? I know that, as a scouter, I've camped close to 600 nights under the stars. Most adult scouters put in about 600 hours of volunteer time a year, as have I. It really is a commitment, but is hugely worthwhile.

Enough reminiscing under the tree, I moved over to my shed. Inside the shed on the right sets a high table. On this table, I have an easel – always with a painting in process, ready for more paint. I think my style of painting is wet oil on wet oil, but I use a lamp to help dry things. I only paint landscapes because my paintings look like a heavy dose of fractal geometry. My tree limbs, bushes, and roads have many different pieces flying in many directions. They look rough and, yet complex.

"Well," I said quietly to myself, "it has been a very long trip from West Virginia to Rincon, Georgia. A long and adventurous trip."

How had I completed this journey without losing my mind or becoming a drug addict, or drinking myself to death? How had I survived those memories of Vietnam?

Years after my two tours in Vietnam, when I was stationed in the Air National Guard as a reservist, my commander of the 165th Airlift Wing once said to me, "Ken, I've figured out how you get things done. You are a 'reductionist.' You take complex problems and break them apart into manageable pieces, or reduce the problem down to simpler solutions, and you achieve your goal."

I was pretty shocked at this, but he accurately identified how I think. Yes, I am a reductionist. Perhaps that comes from my time as an intelligence analyst with both the US Army and the Georgia Air National Guard. This is what I did before I became the chief of staff and, eventually, Vice Commander of the 165th Airlift Wing's Support Group.

On completing my tours in Vietnam, as an analyst with the Army Security Agency in Vietnam, I was assigned as an instructor with the US Army Intelligence Department of Combat Intelligence Order of Battle School at Fort Holabird, Maryland. While there, I taught analysis and the art of contrast and comparison, concepts I understood very well. It was during this assignment that I was introduced to a young lady, my future wife, by my aunt in Florida.

My dear aunt, Dawn Marie, wrote a sweet letter explaining she had a friend that would like to write me. This friend was not dating anyone and had no boyfriend. She was twenty-two and so was I. I had written to so many girls, with little to no results. I was still single, lonely, and without a girlfriend. I wrote back to Aunt Dawn Marie, "If she writes first, then I'll write her, but she has to write the first letter." I wrote this because so many times I had written the first letter to a girl, but eventually the correspondence fell off to nothing, leaving me disappointed and with a lonely heart. *Yep,* I thought, *if that girl really wants to write me, she will write the first letter.* Lo and behold, in less than a week I received a letter from Sandi Bardell. I was impressed.

Sandi sent a picture of herself in her first letter. I still have that picture (now faded) of Sandi sitting on an organ bench, playing her favorite tunes. I noticed her every feature, especially her eyes, which were beautiful. She was tall and slim, with long legs and a pretty smile, and those beautiful eyes. She also enclosed a high school photo of herself which I carried in my wallet for decades until I was afraid it would tear apart. Yes, I found her attractive, and appealing.

Thinking back, what she saw in me is another story. I was skinny, tall and lanky. I had a sense of humor that tended to fall into the range of obnoxious. She didn't know about the one-track mind, or the amount of frivolous data I kept in my brain, most of it about my home state, West Virginia. My best joke, *I thought*, was telling someone if they flattened West Virginia like a pancake, it would be larger than Alaska, a joke that always got an eye roll or a cold shoulder. Needless to say, I wrote back to her and the writing flurry began.

Sandi loved sending cards. Every week I received three or four cards, perfumed no less, and with a letter inside. Her letters weren't mushy, but were concerned about how I was. How was work? Was I well? Her church continued to pray for me even though I had returned from Vietnam in one piece, physically. Those prayers probably helped because, at that time, I was starting to feel the affects of PTSD (Post Traumatic

Stress Disorder), a syndrome that was affecting almost every Vietnam veteran.

For me, it seemed that both going to war and the trip back to home happened so fast that there just wasn't enough time to reflect on where I was going and what I had left behind. On my return, I went from wearing jungle fatigues in Vietnam to street clothes at home in the states – in just three days. It seemed that, back home, nobody cared about where I'd been or what I'd done. So, Sandi's church praying for me was a good thing, and I was impressed with her wisdom and caring that was pouring out through those letters.

Letters turned to phone calls and the voice on the other end of the phone sounded angelic. The Fort Holabird school building had banks of phone booths on the first floor. It was from there I would call her number and charge the bill to my Dad's phone in West Virginia. The operator would call my parents and ask if I could charge my call, and of course, they always said *yes*.

One weekend, when I was home with my parents and brothers my dad asked me, "Kenny, who is it that you make an $80 phone call to every Friday and Saturday?"

"Well…" I explained to Dad about a girl I was writing to. And that she was my aunt's friend.

Dad shook his head and said, "I don't really care, but I wanted to know how you could stay on a phone for so long. Now I think I understand."

I explained to Dad who Sandi was and about how pretty she was and about the cards she sent me. Dad grinned and shook his head in approval and that was my signal that it was okay.

The cards and letters became comfortable and loving. I fell in love through those letters and calls. We knew more about each other before we actually met than anyone can imagine. My grandfather lived in New Port Richey, Florida. Sandi lived near to U.S. 19 in Dunedin, a few miles south of Newport Richey. At that time, I had never traveled south, just east and west. Florida was a place of palm trees and beaches full of bikini-clad girls, and a sun that was as hot and brutal as Vietnam's. That was my perception of Florida–I had a lot to learn.

In January, I received my mandatory reenlistment briefing at Fort Holabird. If I reenlisted, I would be promoted to Staff Sergeant (E-6), but I knew my MOS (Military Occupation Skill) would send me back to Vietnam for another year, a fact pointed out by the recruiter. I refused his offer and I let my Time in Service end (ETS). I was discharged on January 23, 1971, a Friday, and left for home the following day.

The drive from Baltimore, Maryland to Nitro, West Virginia was tedious. I decided to take the northern route along the Pennsylvania turnpike and turn south on US 19 for Charleston. More than 600 miles south on this highway was a girl waiting to see me. We had talked about perhaps my taking a trip south, but nothing was set in stone and I needed to talk to my grandparents first. I thought about these things as I finally hit US 19 and headed south toward Nitro.

The U.S. 19 route is curvy and twists through the Allegheny foothills and mountains. Some turns are so sharp you would think that the taillights you saw ahead were actually from your own car. Finally, after several hours of attacking hills and gliding down the other side, I hit the city of Clendenin and knew I was nearing home. Snaking my way into Charleston I made my way to Sattes, then Nitro, and finally home.

I was out. I was finished. Once home with all the congratulations having been received, I sat in my room for a long time, wondering what would I do next. Life was going to get really hectic the next week.

Sunday, I went up to Humphrey's United Methodist Church to visit and see if anyone attended that I would recognize. I saw no one I remembered; for me it was a lonely church service. I went home feeling I needed to make a change, but the catalyst wasn't cast yet.

On Monday morning, Mom caught me loafing around and asked me what was I going to do. I was without a job, a paycheck, and spent my time goofing off. Mom questioned whether I was able to go back and reclaim my old job.

"No, Mom, that rule only applies to those who were drafted." I said.

"You were drafted, Kenny, I have the draft notice!"

"No, Mom, I joined the US Army, which made the draft notice void."

This went on for a little bit longer, after which, I got up and drove to town to visit anyone or anyplace that might have someone that remembered me. There wasn't. I saw no one who even knew me, much less cared that I'd served my country for three years in the US Army, including two tours in Vietnam.

That night, I called my grandfather (Pop) and Sandi in Florida. Pop agreed to let me stay with them for a long spell. I called Sandi and we discussed what her true feelings were and whether I should I come visit. For me, it was a good time to visit as I was out of work and just moping around.

She answered an enthusiastic "Yes!" to my question. After I got off the phone, I decided to go to Florida. My plan for the trip was to beat a snowstorm moving in from Chicago.

On Tuesday, I pulled all my money from the Nitro Bank and I paid off my sunset red Volkswagen Karmann Ghia coupe. The remaining $650 dollars I pocketed. I told Dad I would start paying my bills from Pop's address in Florida. I put in a forwarding address at the Post Office and ran a few more errands, preparing myself for a very long drive to New Port Richey, Florida.

Wednesday, I packed up what clothes I might need. I used my old Samsonite suitcase and my duffel bag. The inside of that little Volkswagen was getting filled up quickly. Our family dog, Cubby, was following me everywhere I went. I wish I had taken him with me, but Pop had a dog, and Cubby was David and Dana's dog, too (David and Dana being my younger brothers). He was the sweetest dog and cuddled with me every chance he got.

Everything was in place by early Thursday morning. I said my goodbyes to Mom and Dad, David and Dana, and lit out for Florida. My route would take me through the best roads available in 1971. I headed west towards Franklin Kentucky, then south on Interstate 75 towards Knoxville, Tennessee. There was only one problem – it began snowing big heavy snowflakes. Soon the roads were covered in snow, and they became icy.

I had great faith in my Volkswagen. It had brought me home one snowy weekend from Baltimore and now I had to fight snow through Kentucky. Just north of Tennessee, the snow abated and the roads became clear and dry, for which I was thankful. I was getting tired.

I drove from the gently rolling hills of Kentucky to the foothills of the Appalachians as I neared Tennessee. Some parts of the interstate were incomplete, and I was on and off the expressway numerous times. I crossed over several large mountain ranges and eased by Knoxville towards Chattanooga and north Georgia. The sun was setting as I crossed the Georgia line and I was bushed. I found an open motel where I could get some much-needed rest. Day one was at an end, and I needed sleep.

The second day began in Georgia's Appalachian foothills and rolled into the traffic terror of Atlanta. I had no knowledge about which lanes to travel in and I was almost nudged off the freeway from being in the wrong lane. I had experienced a lot of traffic in Baltimore and Washington, but Atlanta was a horrible experience. I finally escaped Atlanta, unharmed, and headed south towards Macon and Valdosta. The road was flat and long.

Georgia is a huge state with 159 counties. Each county seat was designed so every citizen would be within a one day ride by horse to the courthouse. I cut through the heart of Georgia, toward Lake City, Florida. When I crossed the Georgia – Florida border, I began looking for palm trees, but there weren't any. As I traveled, all I saw were pine trees planted row upon row, all the way down to Gainesville, Florida.

Near Gainesville, the land spread out into large, open grassy fields and pastures for as far as I could see. Nearing the area south of Ocala, the groves of orange trees began to spring up. Row upon row of orange groves dotted small rolling hills. The drive was pleasant and warm, my windows were down now and all vestiges of cold weather quickly faded away.

As I neared my turnoff for Florida Route 52, I was reminded of a story Sandi mentioned in her directions to Pop and Dawn's house. "Route 52 is supposed to have creatures that run along your vehicle, Ken, and try to open your door." It was late afternoon, not dark, thank goodness for that. I would tackle Route 52 and those lizard people, or whatever they were, in daylight and that made for a more enjoyable ride. As I recollect I was doing well over 75 mph most of the way across Route 52, figuring any lizard that can run that fast could have me for a meal.

As I neared Bayonet point and US 19, turning left I passed by Weeki Wachee, where mermaids swam in ice cold spring water. I wanted to stop, but I pressed on for Pop's house. I passed through New Port Richey, where my Great Uncle Frank had planted many of the palms that lined its streets. Finally I arrived at Pop, Dawn, and my Aunt Dawn Marie's house.

The air was balmy and their house was on a little rise next to the road. Pop showed me around his place and explained to me about his orange and grapefruit trees. A bird of paradise plant was blooming and I was quite impressed. I had just left snow and was now walking around in a short-sleeved shirt looking at flowers in bloom.

Soon after we ate supper, Dawn Marie took me to visit Sandi and her family. That was a terrific visit and I was able to meet this very tall, slender young woman with beautiful eyes. I knew I was in love with her before we met, but now I was positively sure. We had dessert and sat down to speak about my trip and my home state of West Virginia. We exchanged childhood experiences and compared ideas. I was enchanted with her beautiful eyes. This was Friday night, January 29, 1971.

The next day, Saturday, Sandi and I visited Clearwater Beach, a beautiful white sand beach, where I got my first good look at the Gulf of Mexico. The sea had a greenish-blue color to it that day, and it was hot. We walked on the beach for a while and then returned to the car to visit another spot. We crossed several bridges and visited Sand Key Island. In 1971, Sand Key, a barrier island, was covered with Australian Pines. It was a rugged and somewhat remote beach.

Sunday morning, we went to church and spent the day together at Sandi's house. Then on Monday night, we went to Pop's house to have a small birthday party and some cake, as it was my birthday. The next night we ended up at a popular place called Tiki Gardens, which was out on one of the islands near Largo. Old-timers would remember this place as a nice garden walk with large, noisy peacocks roaming freely about. It was a romantic night, a little cool for February second. I walked her under a covered trellis covered with a vine, making it a perfect place to steal a kiss.

As our lips were about to touch, a man carrying a double-barreled shotgun came sauntering by. It startled us, and in a way, I was thinking of knocking him down. He introduced himself and apologized. He was the owner of Tiki Gardens and was looking for a pesky alligator sneaking up on land, chasing his birds. We snickered and laughed about our "bad" luck and then I finally stole that kiss. I asked her to marry me right then and there, and she said *yes*.

I was heart thrilled because I found a person that really loved me for my silliness and all those things that go with a personality that is both good and bad. My slang, my stories, my Mom and Dad and brothers, none of whom she'd yet met; she had said yes to it all. Then I drove her home, I didn't want to ask her dad for her hand in marriage quite yet, but that chore was going to have to be done soon.

Sandi's father had been a member of the Church of the Brethren and had been raised in a strict Amish-like family. His father made him make a choice at age sixteen. He had to either quit school and work on the farm or get out. He left and eventually joined the US Army.

He shared with us some of his experiences from that time. Mr. Bardell was in his teens when he joined the US Army. He was assigned to the transportation corps. He learned to drive trucks and vehicles at Fort Holabird, Maryland. That was quite a coincidence since I had completed my advanced intelligence training there in 1968 and taught there in 1970. I talked about the very large hump in the middle of the flat base. The hump had a road going right up and over it and down the other side. It, apparently, was kept as a training road for truck drivers. Sandi's father told me about driving up and over that hump when we discussed Fort Holabird and Army life. He was surprised it was still there.

He also told me he'd gotten an Indian motorcycle, maybe from the motor pool, I'm not sure, and took it out for a ride. On a straight stretch in Maryland, or somewhere near Baltimore, he opened it up. He said he slowed way down and quit messing around when he went through a red light doing something like 128 miles per hour! I think that was a come-to-reality meeting with his own mind and I'm sure Mr. Bardell kept his foot off that gas the rest of his life.

Well, we quietly told Sandi's Mom about our marriage plans and she was overjoyed, but I still hadn't asked Mr. Bardell for Sandi's hand. I figured time would help me work up my nerve to ask him. In a way, I was intimidated by his very quiet demeanor. He would talk with you in a soft and direct way. He was very friendly and he always listened to what I had to say as we compared hunting ideas and notes, and life up north. The more I spent time with him, the more I loved him as a second father, and I eventually became the son he never had.

About a month later, we went out to a Chinese restaurant. Sandi said this was the first time she had eaten Chinese food, but I had experienced it at Long Binh, in Vietnam. She ordered ribs. I smiled inside. *Ribs in a Chinese restaurant?* I didn't make fun of her at all, because I was falling in love with this beautiful tall girl. Suddenly, as I saw her pull the ribs apart, one of them flipped up in the air and disappeared. We looked for that wayward food, but no rib was to be found. We looked under our table and, still, there was no tell-tale sign of it on her dress or in her lap. It just disappeared and was a mystery. Later that evening, she opened her purse for lipstick, and there it was, a perfect rib, inside her clutch. I couldn't help myself. I had to laugh and shake my head.

Chapter 2

A Pink Shirt–February to August 1971

For several weeks, I loafed around my grandparent's house. I cut grass, helped in the garden, and paid my rent, but pretty much spent my time fishing or just driving around learning the area. I visited Aunt Virgie, the widow of Uncle Frank Luikart. They lived in New Port Richey. Uncle Frank was a botanist, in his own right, and planted all the palms seen in Newport Richey along U.S. 19 today.

Aunt Virgie lived in a small caretaker's cottage attached to a large house. Their son, David, was a pharmacist in New Port Richey, and his sons played basketball for the local high school.

It was always pleasant to sit and just chat with Aunt Virgie. She reminded me of the elderly lady up Morgan's holler, outside of Nitro, who used to leave her door open for us to come in and get warm in the winter, or a cool glass of water in the summer. Aunt Virgie was a sweet lady, and I am all the richer for knowing her. I enjoyed talking with cousin David, comparing notes and talking about my brother, David. Cousin David was a decorated World War II veteran himself. We talked briefly about the Army and how some things were the same and some things had changed. I wish I had spent more time with him.

The time finally came to get a job because the $640 in my newly established bank account in Florida wasn't going to go far. Also, I had to pay for college. I had been accepted for the 1971 fall quarter at Lake City Forest Ranger School, in their Forest Ranger Program (this college had many academic programs). Lake City was about 175 miles north of Dunedin and I would have to stay in a dormitory, which would be tough on a newly wedded couple.

Out-of-state fees, including room and board, would drive the costs each semester close to $900, so I made the decision to go for it and just get it done. I figured I would need about $1,000 per semester to enroll, buy books and live in Lake City. In the spring of 1971, while still living with my grandparents, I started working at Rose's Department Store in Holiday, Florida. I worked long shifts every day. Back then, you didn't make all that overtime you make nowadays, but those long shifts brought in a lot of money. I banked everything and saved enough for the entire year at Forest Ranger School and some for the wedding. Also, while attending Lake City College, I applied for my Veterans Administration School Bill and received $175 a month per every school month I attended. Yes, $175 a month was all a married veteran got for school in 1971.

The evening soon came when I got up the courage needed to ask Dad Bardell for his blessing to marry his daughter. He and I were sitting in their living room. He was rocking quietly and turned off the TV and he started to stand up, heading to bed.

"Umm, sir, I need to ask you a question." I said pensively.

He sat back down and raised his right hand, "Go ahead, Ken, what's on your mind?" he said quietly.

"Mr. Bardell, Sandi and I have been dating and we really enjoy each other's company. She's really the girl I've been looking for all my life. I'd like to ask you if you would give me permission to marry her?"

Dad was quiet for a bit, he always thought an answer through, so I didn't panic. "Ken, I thought you were going to Forest Ranger School? Will this mess up your schooling?"

I smiled and said quietly, "No sir, we have talked it out and she will continue to live here and work while I stay in Lake City our first year. It will be hard on us, but we can make it."

He thought for a minute, smiled, and said, "Yes, as long as you promise to take good care of her." He rose up out of his chair, shook my hand, hugged Sandi, and slipped off to bed. Now we needed to tell her mom, but she already knew. Women know things and talk about things us men never get to be a part of.

My mom was in the dark. I called home regularly but, for the most part, she wasn't involved in this decision making, neither was my Dad. I guess for me it was a big personal step, and one that I wasn't afraid to take because I could work at anything, and make some kind of living. I called Mom that weekend and explained to her I was going to get married. She cried. I guess that was a blow, but I wasn't sure if she was crying for me, or for poor Sandi.

She once jumped on me, "Do you leave all those whiskers in Mrs. Bardell's sink?"

"No Mom." I rolled my eyes. "I don't and I'll clean those up right now." So maybe Mom was crying for Sandi, I don't know, I've never asked her why.

With that, I was prepared to get married on 7th August, 1971. Sandi chose the church and her bridal colors and what she wanted me to wear–a pink shirt with ruffles. Our first controversial discussion, as potential man and wife, was over a man's shirt. "Pink is for sissies!" I told her.

But she countered, "Pink can be worn to match a bridal color and that's what I want, can't you give in a little?" I was a Vietnam Veteran from West Virginia. In the hills, the Appalachians, we don't wear white shorts, and we don't wear anything pink. Blue jeans and shirtless was customary in the summer, but now I was asked to wear pink.

I gave in, and the pink shirt was ordered, along with a white jacket and black trousers. Actually, it didn't look too bad on me. I had two suits with me I had ordered from Hong Kong when I was in Vietnam. Made of shark skin material, the suits, and vests, were tailor made and fit like a glove. I loved the blue suit, and chose it for our getaway clothes after the wedding. We even planned how the car, a 1969 mustang 302, with black interior would be decorated. We had a million plans in motion.

As the day of the wedding approached, Sandi met my parents for the first time. She was stunningly tall, and her skin was silky white with a perfect smile. She had "smiling" eyes. My Dad fell in love with her too, especially after in trying to help him butter some corn she dropped a big pat of soft butter on the tip of his shoe. Dad didn't notice, he was still arranging his plate, but his future daughter-in-law was on the floor wiping his shoe off.

Dad looked down. She smiled and said. "I dropped butter on your toe," and Dad let out a laugh. That was Dad; he was a funny, just, righteous, good man. The ice was broken and now all we had to do was get through the wedding.

Two things I don't like are weddings and funerals. Don't ask me why, but neither of those occasions are happy times for me. I get through them, but it seems like there is a lot to both that separate the attendees from the person being honored. I mean who in his right mind would say, "Oh, doesn't he look so natural? Umm, no, he's dead!"

When “Does anyone here object to this wedding speak now or forever hold your peace,” was said, I always want to shout out, “Get all you ever wanted to buy in your life before you get married! Get that Browning automatic shotgun, or bass boat, or how about a Corvette?” But I digress.

The wedding day had arrived. I am telling you this all happened in our little wedding, and its amazing that we both survived the day. First thing that morning, Sandi’s mom lost the key to the church. She was ready to go decorate, set up everything, and no key. They tore the house up looking for that key. To this day that key has never been found. They went to the pastor to get a spare key, he didn’t have one. Now panic was setting in. He had to call on one of the trustees to open the church up to be decorated. Unfortunately, they had a tough time finding him. Everyone was beginning to panic.

I went ahead and took our suitcases to the Sandpiper Inn at St. Petersburg Beach. On the way back from that little excursion, the brakes went out on Sandi’s car and I had to have it towed over to one of Dad Bardell’s friend’s house. Now I’m down a car, the one that we planned on taking on our trip. I had to stay and help get it fixed. Finally, I got Sandi’s mustang home, the suitcases were in our hotel room, and it seemed like everything was going better.

The day of the wedding, the white aisle runner the princess bride was to walk upon was rolled out and pinned into place. I was in place, my Dad, who was best man, was there and my brother David (who had just received his orders for Vietnam on that day) was there. My youngest brother Dana was there, Mom was there, and Sandi's cousins were there. Those three boys were ornery. I liked them, but I never trusted them to keep from messing up Sandi's mustang.

Finally, the music began. "Here comes the bride." Those words sang in my head. I was sweating up a storm. Sandi was wearing a pearl-studded wedding dress, hand sewn by her mother. She was stunningly beautiful in that dress. The bridesmaids were dressed in pink dresses that matched my shirt. It was quite a sight to behold in that little church near Gulf to Bay Boulevard, outside Clearwater.

On her Dad's arm, Sandi glided smoothly up the aisle and began to climb several steps to where I was waiting. As she climbed the steps, her petticoat caught on one of the straight pins holding the white aisle runner. A ripping and tearing sound occurred under her dress. That unnerved all of us standing at the top of the steps; I expected to see her dress fall off, but it didn't.

The pastor was smiling and looking as though he had everything under control. Unfortunately, right before the ceremony, he had learned his father, in Ohio, was gravely ill. He was going straight to Ohio after our wedding. This news upset him greatly and the sound of Sandi's dress ripping, unnerved him. He began, "Dearly beloved, we are gathered here to join in matrimony Sandra Lynn Bardell to…" After a very long pause, then he stammered, “Sandra to” I whispered “Ken Luikart, to Ken Luikart.” Then from that point on, he totally forgot what we had agreed upon for the wording of our ceremony. He just had to adlib it to the end, forgetting that an organist of fame we hired to play at our wedding was totally forgotten about. She never played the music we picked out, because he forgot to pause for her to play at the agreed upon time.

Regardless, we were married in the eyes of God, and our families. We finally moved to the proverbial cutting of the cake and the bride throwing her bouquet. After that exercise we dressed to go on our honeymoon. Dad slipped me a pair of wire cutters, and he paid the preacher for me.

Outside, Sandi’s cousins were busy decorating her car, as requested, except for one major detail. They put copious amounts of car wax on the door handle of the driver’s side. We ran out under a hail of rice, which was later cleaned up so that not one bird died. I seated Sandi in the car and slid around to the other side to get in, where the crowd pushed me up against the driver’s door smashing all that car wax across the front of my pants. Creating an embarrassing waxy chunky mess and ruined them for further use. That was a $300 suit, 1969 money; it was now ruined for my honeymoon. I was not happy about that.

The rest of the honeymoon went on as usual as those things go, except for two incidents. The first thing that happened was to Sandi’s cousins after the wedding.

Once things had been cleaned up at the church, they decided to go get something to eat. After changing their clothes and leaving their young children with relatives, they set out. They hadn't gone very far when they were stopped by Clearwater police and held for a bit. It seems there had been an abduction of a baby in South Carolina. The cousins had the same make and model of the car with South Carolina plates that had been used in the kidnapping. And to make matters worse, in the back of their car was diapers and some baby bottles.

The policeman stopped them and asked, "Where is the baby?" Whereupon the youngest cousin, who thought he was being funny, spouted off that they'd left the baby in the trunk. They were all made to sit on the side of the road. Finally, after numerous phone calls, the police figured out they had the wrong people. Fortunately, their kids were being watched by Sandi's mom and aunt. I think that was providence that they had to sit on the side of the road until positive identification was made.

The second incident happened in St. Augustine, Florida. At the Ponce De Leon Hotel we were given a room on the third floor. That night, we were the only guests on the entire floor. The hotel brought us wine and cheese and it was really a pleasant stay. Our first night there was romantic and sweet.

The next morning, we wanted to sleep in a bit. We were both tired and mentally drained. Meanwhile, the Florida Pest Control guy showed up to spray rooms in the hotel for bugs. He was told that we were the only people on the third floor and to leave us alone. After treating all the other rooms, he decided to enter our room with a pass key, knocking as he opened the door.

He walked in to see what he could see, but I jumped out of bed and did a rebel yell scream at him. He dropped his sprayer and took off running. I chased him down the hall, buck naked, wishing to tear his head off, but he beat me to the fire escape door and was gone. As I ran out of the room, I heard the door slam shut. The words, "I'm locked out" screamed in my brain. I didn't care, until I started to go downstairs for a talk, then I decided I'd better return, knock, and get some clothes on.

I returned, dressed, and took the bug man's sprayer to the manager's office. I requested that he let me return the sprayer in person, but the manager said, "No, don't do that. I'll give you another night's stay for free." I agreed and went back to room to cool down.

We had a fun and uneventful honeymoon, except Sandi sat on my sunglasses, and three kids ended up in our honeymoon photo shot at Silver Springs. We still don't know where they came from. As soon as a person agreed to take our picture, three kids, I think they were his, ran up and stood with us. Now we had gained three children.

We also were the only people I ever heard of to get stuck in the sand while driving on Daytona Beach. We had to be towed out of that one. Maybe our honeymoon wasn't uneventful after all. We had fun and arrived home prepared to face life together. A team – a man and wife, so poor, and destitute, that the accountant laughed at our combined salary for 1971. He said, "You're probably several thousands of dollars below poverty level!" We knew, *we knew.*

With Sandi living at home and me living in Lake City in Granger Hall, our friends made bets we would be divorced in less than a year. But time proved that love can conquer all, and that sacrifice can sometimes make love stronger.

CHAPTER 3

Follow the Trail of the Timber Wolf; Lake City, FL. 1971–1973

I attended Lake City Forest Ranger School and Community College, a very long name, that was changed in 1974 to Lake City Community College. This school was one of the best schools in the east for training to be a Forest Ranger, also known as a Forest Technician. It was a small college located east of Lake City, Florida, along Highway 90.

Surrounding Lake City Community College were old growth planted pines. Slash, Loblolly, and Longleaf pines stood tall and erect around the college. Looking like the walls of a fortress, the pines were impressive.

The college campus was small so it was simple to walk from one building to the next in less than five minutes. Even Granger Hall, a small X-shaped dormitory, was close to our main classroom #135 in Galloway Hall. Galloway Hall was a wedge-shaped building with stair stepped seating inside. Most of our classes were held in this room.

The college had a pretty good basketball team, known as the Timber Wolves. School dress standards were fairly strict: shirts were tucked in, no pants with holes, and no shorts. Haircuts were mandatory and beards were not allowed, which were cited as a fire risk during classes on fire fighting.

While the Forest Ranger School was not a military school, the tough standards and classes culled out a lot of students. No women were admitted in our class of 72 men. They were forbidden to take this course. The classes on dendrology (tree identification) and forest mensuration (forest math for cruising timber) reduced our class after two and a half years from 72 men to 28. All 28 men were hired right out of school after graduating. That was the gift you received for enduring a very physically tough and mentally brutal school.

Going back to school at age 23 was awkward. I wasn't the only veteran in the class. Dean S., a former postal employee, and Tom S. were both Navy veterans. All of us were older than most of the other students in college. I was one of the unfortunate married students who lived in Granger Hall. Living near teenage students tested your endurance for noise and silliness.

One evening, one of my fellow classmates caught a snake. Now, I've learned to leave snakes alone. Just leave them alone and they will leave you alone. But here he came into Granger Hall carrying a long reptile, all coiled around his arm. One of the Liberal Arts students, whose name but not his face escapes me, joined in the excitement of having a snake in the dorm. I was getting pretty bored with all of this and was about to retire to bed when the Liberal Arts student stuck his finger into the front of the snake's mouth and quipped "Is he poisonous?" The snake struck the boy on the index finger so quickly, grabbing onto it and nailing him hard, that the snake charmer dropped him. Right in the middle of Granger Hall, we had an unknown type of snake on the loose, coiled and ready to strike again, and no one was around. I mean the hall vacated instantly. The Liberal Arts guy howled and screamed, "I'm gonna die! I'm gonna die! I'm gonna die!" and ran from one end of the hall to the other. Friends were trying to catch him, while the snake handler got his bearings and attempted to round up the snake again. Of course, there was never a shovel or a hoe nearby when you need one.

When the panicked young man was captured, and the snake was under control again, friends took him and the snake to Lake City Hospital. Fortunately, it was just a blacksnake, but it did have teeth and it left him with a sore finger, and was given a tetanus shot. We made a new rule that night, no more snakes will be brought into the dormitory. To me that rule made sense, much more sense than the placard in the bathroom that read, "Flush Twice – It's a Long Way to The Cafeteria."

I would bet today's dorm students would find all of us a bit more old fashioned, as the big game in the dorm was a never ending game of RISK. We had teams and every night we played the board game for two hours or more until it got late and we got tired. Huge battles were fought over many nights and I'm surprised that fights didn't erupt over the intensity we brought to the game. Everyone behaved and took their losses like a gentleman.

My roommate was Ron P., who was from Alabama. He was enrolled in the Aircraft Maintenance School. I think the school officials roomed us together because we were similar in age. The food at the cafeteria was about all there was available. There was a beer joint down the road, mostly rednecks and locals, and the root beer place down on U.S. Highway 441. In 1971, there wasn't much variety in Lake City. If you traveled a few miles east you came to Olustee, Florida. It had a beer joint and some houses. It was the home of the U.S. Forest Service Naval Stores Research Facility which conducted studies of turpentine and turpentine methods.

We were taught that every tree could have two faces. A face is a lateral scrape across the front or back of the tree, putting a tin run off trough and a metal square pan to catch the gum. After you made the scrape, you used sulfuric acid to make the tree bleed and, after a few days, the pans were gathered and scraped into a turpentine barrel. Our instructor, Professor M, emphasized you needed 10,000 faces to make a crop. In 1971, a crop could almost make you a year's salary. 10,000 faces equaled 5,000 trees. Do the math, if you have roughly

500 trees per acre, because these are older trees, and it is more open, you would need about ten acres of land. Most people had more than one crop.

The only turpentine factory I ever visited was near Valdosta, Georgia. The plant processed pine tree gum and produced turpentine. Each landowner was paid according to the cleanliness of the gum. Today most everyone would be appalled at how this was accomplished. I put it here solely as historical information. I don't condone it, don't support how they did this, but this is the truth. I witnessed it first-hand. Gum cleanliness was determined by the color of the gum. The darker the gum, the more material was suspended in the gum. It was worth less than clear gum.

A sample was drawn and smeared on a piece of glass. The glass was held up to an opaque color stick. On this stick were various shades of black. The name on the stick was associated with the colors black people call themselves – High Yellow, Whiten, Red Bone, etc. The way they named the tones kind of shocked me, and I was somewhat taken aback at how flagrantly open this type of grading was carried out. But, this was 1973, and civil rights had a long way to go.

During the winter, we would volunteer to string fire through the woods for the U.S. Forest Service in the Olustee National Forest. I remember taking a fire drip torch and, following a straight line, I made a fire break, trailing fire for one or two miles. Others followed to make sure the fire was headed in the right direction, but burning in January and February meant steady winds from the north.

Burning the forest is necessary in the south. It was something the Indians did every year, and it kept bad fires down and created a growing climate for the Longleaf Pine tree. You needed a steady wind, from the north, a very cold day (as this would keep from damaging the pine trees, but kill brush and hardwoods) and a plan for controlling the burn.

I ride around many areas near Savannah today, and I see understory (brush) 15' high. Most of the timber companies sold their timberland for development. Owners that bought the land were not interested in fire control; they only saw money in land development. If you rode down any side road near Savannah you'd see huge warehouses, and strip malls, and housing developments. All of these properties are bordered by timberland with heavy underbrush. A lot of people look at the lush green growth under the pine trees and just see bugs and stickers. I see gasoline.

That green stuff will burn like you'd thrown gas on a fire. Most of those species of underbrush will burn with great intensity, especially under conditions of a warm day, and wrong-direction of winds. A wind pushing a fire is dangerous. After a large fire destroyed many homes in Florida, I wondered what was on the minds of the forestry people who set the fire. It was the month of May, variable winds, it was hot, and the underbrush was about 15' high. With these conditions, someone lit a fire to burn off brush. It burned down entire housing developments. This has happened more than once in South Georgia and North Florida. Fires swept through the Okefenokee Swamp and could end up burning underground for months. Some fires burn so fast and so hot that firebreaks several football fields wide cannot stop it.

I made a passing remark about using a helicopter that flings out ping-pong balls injected with a substance that catches fire after hitting the ground. All the balls ignite at once, causing the numerous little fires to burn toward each other, thus burning a much larger area of understory, and creating a fire break miles wide instead of yards wide. I guess it was too unstable a situation, but they couldn't stop the fires' head anyway. Why not try something that allowed them to jump way ahead of a fire and get something backfired that might work?

So, with the Florida fire, I asked a question of a fire fighter, "Why do they light a fire in terrible conditions?" His answer was, "Because they have people sitting idle that don't have a fire to fight, if it gets out of control they have something to do." Well, that's kind of damning if you think about it, but in a way it makes sense. No forest ranger, in his right mind, sets a fire to the woods to burn off a 15' high understory in May, when winds are extremely variable, when it's hot, near people and houses. I wouldn't. I'll let that stand on it's own.

School had its lighter moments. Every class had a class clown. Jimbo W. was one of those young men. He was always doing something silly or daring. One hot humid afternoon, a group of students put together a bet that Jimbo wouldn't roll in a mud hole before class. A dollar was collected from each participant and shown to him. "Go roll in that mud hole and we will give you every dollar you see here." I guessed it was about $15 dollars. Immediately he jumped from the porch of our classroom building and ran straight for the mud hole. Without hesitation, he dropped and rolled to and fro across a nasty mud hole, making the dark milky water splash. After rolling for a minute he jumped up, shook off the muddy clumps of dirt, dripping wet with chocolate-colored water, he came back on the porch and collected his money. The teacher asked "What happened to you?"

He just replied, "I was on my way here and slipped and fell in a mud hole." The class erupted in laughter and somewhat of a cheer. The teacher, dumbfounded, shook his head and turned to the blackboard. It was time for class.

We had some of the best instructors during my two and a half years of school. Mr. M. taught dendrology. He often talked about the grumbling he heard from some of the students about how rough the woods were. Briars, marsh, and heavy undergrowth made cruising timber difficult. Mr. M. would stand before us, hold his hands together and say, "You really don't know how hard you have it until you wake up in the morning and your sleeping bag is encrusted in ice and snow. When I was in World War II, I broke the ice a many a morning during the Battle of the Bulge." And that was about all he said about our misery. In other words, suck it up or quit.

We had to learn about 350 trees, including their scientific names. Learning to correctly pronounce and write scientific names was tough for a West Virginia boy who still spoke a lot of hill pronunciations. But in time, I learned those names. My favorite scientific tree name is Melia Azedarach, or the China Berry. Think you haven't seen a China Berry? Well it's planted all around old farms, houses, and barns in the south. Those tall trees with small leaflets on a compound leaf are China Berry trees. They are everywhere. I always thought a daughter named Melia Azerdarach Luikart would be the cat's meow! I know one girl who is glad that never happened.

We spent many hours cruising timber in the Osceola National Forest. It lies north of Lake City along US Highway 90. It was massive; some of it was swamp and tough to penetrate. Sometimes we would help them burn the forest off to remove undergrowth, other times we cruised timber on some of their tracts to practice our cruising skills. This proved to be extremely tough as we sometimes had to bust through a swamp filled with water.

On one such cruising exercise, I was with two other young men. We were warned of bears and alligators, which made creeping through a swamp tedious, causing the hair on the back of our necks to stand up. Ti Ti and wax myrtle were interspersed between stretches of water where nothing lived. You could not see your boots, or the floor of the wet pond. It was just cold water.

We stopped to rest when I heard a noise. "What's that? I asked. Everyone froze for an instant. The forest was quiet.

"I don't hear anything," my buddy Dean S. said. We trudged on a few more feet and stopped to take a bearing shot. "Darn, I hear it now!" he said in a low voice. All three of us stopped, froze and listened. Nothing was moving or making a sound. Then again we heard it. "What is that?" Dean said looking around his body. It was close on us.

Our third buddy said, "What, this?" and we heard a scrunching noise like a drowning toad.

"Yeah, what the heck is that?" I said.

Finally our buddy said, "It's just a sound made by my toes in my socks, with my boots full of water. I guess I gotta try to drain it out."

We made our way to a tree log and all three of us stood up on the log facing the same way. The third guy's boot, on his right foot, had a perfectly round hole in the toe. As he stood on the log it was peeing water out the hole and all three of us almost fell off the log laughing.

When I was young, I thought forestry was following Little Bunny Foo Foo through the woods, studying his living habits and helping squirrels survive and taking care of deer. But that was not the case at all. It was a business. A business of wood and formulas. I had stepped into the minefield of math, all kinds of math, formulas and factoring, cruising timber and working predictive cords per acre for someone selling their timber. Forest surveying, silviculture, tree species to site locations, and how to remove nuisance trees, firefighting, and so on, I was feeling overwhelmed.

I kept my nose in the books and actually studied. This was aided by my time with the US Army and work as an Intelligence Analyst. I was getting the math, understanding the formulas and working tough problems. I even learned how to close up a survey by using latitudes and departures, by hand. I was very pleased with my ability to finally handle math, and felt like it was possible to teach an old dog new tricks.

Our last half of school lasted through the summer months and ended right before September. This was our six-week training course. We were broken up into teams and taken to different forest companies, the US Forest Service, the Florida Forest Service, the Georgia Fire Lab in Valdosta, and a week-long adventure on a raft, living off the land while floating down the Santa Fe, then the Suwannee rivers. All I took was my sleeping bag, a tarp, a knife, some drinking water, and a small backpack with waterproof matches and one change of clothes.

We put in at a bridge over the Santa Fe River. Our raft held our instructor and about five other men. It was substantial, but heavy and bulky. It floated on 55 gallon drums and had a plywood deck. As soon as we worked our way to the center of the river we rigged an underwater sail. We spread a tarp so the stream pushed the raft faster downstream. This moved us at a pretty good pace.

The five nights of camping varied from a nice, picnic-like spot to eking out a spot big enough to pitch a tent. We captured a rattlesnake one night and cooked it up for supper. Honest it tasted like chicken and we ate all of it, minus the bones. I would not recommend that now days as rattlesnakes are a protected species, I believe.

We ate berries and fish as we floated down the river. We passed numerous blue holes that filled the river with crystal clear water, but after mixing with the dark water of the Suwannee, it was no longer clear. The dark water is a result of all the tannic acid from trees along the river. Some people drink the dark tea, some use it to heal wounds. I believe it helps to heal wounds, but I would not drink a lot of tannic acid water.

After floating down the Suwannee for many miles, we finally came to our takeout point. This was the last week long training episode of 1973. I returned to school, finished my finals, and graduated with a 3.62 grade average. I was finally on the Dean's List! Sandi also graduated from Lake City with an Associate of Arts degree. We were the first husband and wife to graduate together, specifically, the first husband and wife to graduate at the same time. Now it was time to find a job and get busy making a living and a life together.

CHAPTER 4

Into the Dark Veld–1973

How I ended up in Georgia is a story of chance. During the graduation week at Lake City, I applied to Weyerhaeuser Forest Company, the US Forest Service, and the Florida Forest Service in Pinellas County, Florida. I wanted a job in Florida, or perhaps North or South Carolina. I was called by Weyerhaeuser and scheduled an interview a week after graduation. Meanwhile, I was interviewed by the US Forest Service and Florida Forestry.

Florida Forestry didn't pan out, but the US Forest Service said they would get back to me. Meanwhile, I prepared for my interview in Jacksonville, North Carolina. We loaded our dog and headed north. The company paid for two nights at a local motel, and we tried to have a positive outlook on life in Jacksonville. I was tired and went to bed early. I had a 9:00 A.M. meeting with their woodlands manager the next morning. I dressed and had breakfast and drove to their plant, then to the woodlands building.

The interview went well and he volunteered the following information. I would be required to work extremely long hours on a fire plow. That job possibly included sleeping on the plow in the woods, for $2.00 an hour. That was okay money, but a college education wasn't needed to fill that job. I told him I needed to think about the offer a little longer. He agreed and I left.

Sandi and I talked about the offer, which was pretty low wages for a college graduate, but the long hours on a fire plow plus sleeping in the woods during fire season was not appealing. Even though Westvaco (West Virginia Pulp and Paper Company) was a homegrown timber company, Weyerhaeuser was the company I had always wanted to work for.

On the return trip home, we stopped in Beaufort, South Carolina, at Sandi's aunt and uncle's house for a couple of nights. While talking about the offer from Weyerhaeuser, Aunt Jane mentioned Union Camp Paper Corporation. *Union Camp?* That company never crossed my mind but I was close by. I thought, *Why not call them in the morning and see what they had to offer?*

The next morning I called their office in Savannah and they asked me to come in for a short interview and to fill out an application. I did, and was asked if I would work out of Rincon, Georgia. I said, "I've never visited Rincon, what's there?" They answered, "Our Woodlands Research department is located in Rincon." I agreed to go visit Rincon and talk with a Mr. Harry

B. I received instructions on how to get there and off I went up Georgia Highway 21 to Rincon, Georgia.

As soon as I left the traffic circle at Garden City headed for Rincon, I was in woods. Almost the entire twenty miles or so to Rincon was wooded with pine trees, on both sides of the road. Before the county line, in Chatham County, was a rundown old church on my right. Later on men from Rincon United Methodist Church rebuilt that church.

There was a bar at the Chatham and Effingham county line. It looked tough; and later I actually found out it was as tough and rough a place as it looked. Several more miles up the road and I climbed up a steep little hill and past an old Methodist Church, Goshen Methodist. The small wood-frame church looked well over a hundred plus years old. The bar and the church were the first structures I saw on my way to Rincon.

Soon, I passed a housing development that was fairly modern. This was Westwood Heights. The road dipped into Swiegoffer Creek and shortly afterward, I passed over Willowpeg Creek, then uphill slightly to the Woodlands Research Office building where the current-day Kroger parking lot is currently located. The woodlands building was a wooden structure, white with green shutters. Behind the building were company gas tanks and beyond these lay a large pine tree seed orchard.

I parked the car in the parking lot and walked into the back door, and met their secretary, Mrs. Wilma C.

She introduced me to Mr. M., Mr. B., and Mr. Z. Finally, I met Mr. Harry B., the forester that was going to hire a technician to work in their ditch and drainage projects. We sat down and Mr. B. laid out all the jobs I would be exposed to: planting trees for different projects, measuring growth and yield plots, fertilization studies, working with the superior tree program, collecting pine cones at harvest time for their superior tree program, conducting studies along ditches cut by Union Camp to find any growth spurts, and so on. There were so many different jobs to do, something different every day. I liked this concept of being busy and working in many aspects of forest research.

Living in Rincon would be a requirement. If I accepted their offer, he would have Union Camp move my mobile home from Lake City, Florida, to Rincon, Georgia, and set it back up. Also, he gave me a starting salary of $3.50 an hour, with an immediate raise if I passed my trial period. I told him I would let him know within the week. I needed to confer with Sandi. He agreed, and we shook hands and I left him with the understanding that I wanted the job. Later that week, I called him and accepted the position. That was how I ended up in Rincon, Georgia.

Rincon was a small town with large lots for each house. Our trailer was going to be placed in Boyd's trailer park, behind the SOC gas station and across from the Red and White grocery store. Mr. B. had planted numerous dogwood and red bud trees, it was both quiet and beautiful in the spring.

The streets of Rincon were tree lined and very shady. A bike ride in Rincon could be taken without ever leaving the shade, even if you crossed Highway 21, you remained in shade. It was a quiet town with "blue laws" on Sunday. Nothing was open on Sunday, or Wednesday afternoon. All stores were closed. In addition, Effingham County was a "dry" county. No beer or alcohol was sold in any store, gas station, or eating establishment. There were no bars in Rincon, no honky-tonk places, no juke joints. You had to go to the county line or the Swamp Fox, down on Highway 30, for a beer.

People in Savannah had no clue as to where Rincon was, even though Effingham County and Savannah had a relationship since the 1700's. Savannah had garments, silk, tea, and sugar, and so on; Effingham County had milk, meat, sausage, eggs and poultry. A lot of trading was done by barter back then and the two communities – one Austrian and German, the other English – served each other well. Effingham had great stability. The families that had lived here for centuries still owned the same properties. Some lived in the same homes and farmed the same land as their ancestors.

We were at home in Lake City, when the truck arrived to take our trailer away to Rincon. As the trailer left for Georgia, we picked up our mail for the last time on our way out of town. As I watched our green trailer make a turn onto the highway, I opened a letter from the US Forest Service. The letter read "Dear Kenneth, you have been chosen to work with the US Forest Service as a GS-5. You will need to report to the Osceola National Forest to fill out paperwork to become a member of the US Forest Service." I was awarded a GS 5 with the Forest Service. My dream had come true, however, I was already on a different path, a dream of becoming a Forest Technician for Union Camp Paper Corporation.

The day after Labor Day, 1973, I started working for Union Camp. Immediately, I was immersed into a very tough schedule, driving a company truck. We would travel 200 miles a day to complete a job; thus began my career in forestry.

Soon after beginning my new job, Sandi's Mustang needed an oil change. I took it to Burns Gulf station and left the keys. I asked the attendant for an oil change and all lubricants to be updated or checked, and off I went to Robertsville, South Carolina.

According to a historical sign, Robertsville, Jasper County, South Carolina, was the home town of Henry Martyn Robert, born May 2, 1837. He was a US Army General and Chief of Engineers. He published the first book on *Roberts' Rules of Order* in 1876 (Wikipedia, 30 July, 2018).

There isn't much in Robertsville. It's a crossroads with a post office and some antebellum homes. As a matter of fact, Jasper County was one of the poorest counties in the nation. When General Sherman reached Savannah, Georgia, he rearmed and refurbished his troops, then headed towards South Carolina, burning everything in his path. He was brutal, and he even burned Charleston, S.C. to the ground. He claimed it was an accident, but Charleston is where the war began. Sherman made sure Charleston paid the price for that transgression – in his mind, at least.

Looking around after reading the historical sign in Robertsville, there just wasn't much to see. The home town of the man that wrote *Roberts Rules of Order* was just a crossroad in a rural county. We finished our growth and yield measurements and headed back to Rincon. South Carolina has a preponderance of ticks. Riding in the truck, I could feel them crawling up my legs, under my armpits, on my back and yikes – some were attached. It was a miserable trip home.

When we arrived home, I went to pick up my car from the Gulf station, the owner looked at me and asked, "Who are you?" He had never seen me before in Rincon and he was not going to change oil on someone's car with Florida tags that he didn't recognize. No, he didn't change my oil, but if I brought it back the next day it would get done first thing. Now that he knew where I lived and who I worked for, all was copacetic. I drove her car home, still itchy from ticks and asked her to meet me at the back door with a plastic garbage bag.

This became a regular routine. I would strip down to my boxer shorts, place all my clothes in the bag. I would leave my boots outside until I could spray them. I would go into the bathroom, fill the tub with Clorox water and step into the tub. Then began the arduous task of pulling ticks off of my body. Sandi would check the backside and continue to pull ticks off until all were removed. I would then finish with a shower and put on clean clothes. Meanwhile, Sandi started the washer and immediately washed my clothes. This happened almost every day while I worked for Union Camp in the woods.

Union Camp was an interesting company. At one time, Savannah had the largest digester for making pulp and paper in the world. They sold that sometime after International Paper acquired the company in the early 1990s. At the Savannah Airport, I saw it loaded on an AN-124, the largest airplane in the world. The digester was headed to Russia. At that time, the Savannah plant hired about 3,000 plus people. After the takeover by International Paper and ensuing reduction of mills and employees, the plant had about 700 people working. Back in the 70s, Union Camp was the number one employer in the area, except for perhaps the 24th Infantry Division at Fort Stewart. Union Camp had three large regions, Georgia (Georgia, Florida, South Carolina), Alabama (Autauga County in the northern portion, and Chapman Alabama in the southern part), and Virginia (three large areas along three rivers, Nansemond, Nottoway, and Meherrin).

The Georgia region had eleven forests. They were named after rivers traversing the area of operations. All these rivers had been named for local Native American tribes. The Ohoopee, Oconee, Ocmulgee, Combahee, Ogeechee, Altamaha, Satilla, Sapelo, Suwannee, Okefenokee, and Seminole were each a river named after a specific tribal nation. Each forest was approximately 100,000 acres in size. The forest was broken down into 35,000 acre working circles named after local landmarks or former tract landowners. Inside each working circle, there were approximately seven 5,000 acre compartments. The forest had one forest supervisor, and he may have had an assistant or two. Each working circle would have one or two forest technicians. That was the total workforce on the Forest side of things.

All totaled, Union Camp had about 1.1 million acres in Georgia, 300,000 acres in Virginia, and about 250,000 acres in Alabama. In my fourteen years working with the research department, I got to see almost all of this land. Here is a listing of all the areas of research where I worked in. I know this is perhaps boring to the reader, but I add this for historical records, as it will be lost forever in a few more years.

Check out the following project numbers;

WA = Allowed Time	WN = Admin activities
WR 1 = Fertilization studies	WR 2 = Hardwood improvement
WR 3 = Pine tree improvement	WR 4 = Hybrid studies
WR 6 = Growth and Yield Study	WR 17 = Drainage Studies
WCR 3 = Forest Service high density study	WCR 8 = Hardwood Growth and Yield study
WCR 11 = Fomes Annosus Study (root rot)	WCR 16 = Site Quality study
WCR 25 = Insect attack studies	WCR 26 = Paraquat study (making standing lighter wood)
WTSR 5 = Seed Harvester study	WTSR 9 = Peeled wood study
WS 5 = Equipment maintenance	WS 7 = Grounds cleanup

Every day was a different task. Sometimes with several different tasks on land hundreds of miles apart. We tried to schedule our trips to be thrifty with time, but usually we spent one to three nights out of town each week. My working days were long, at least ten hours, or daylight until dark. That schedule drained your body. At that time I was probably 140 pounds soaking wet. We figured each day we walked approximately ten miles over rugged, rough terrain, jumping creeks, all while watching for hidden wells and stump holes. You could definitely die by falling in a well or end up with a broken leg from stepping into a stump hole.

Snakes were worrisome, but hogs were to be feared. A female with babies could go stark raving mad and attack you until it killed you, or you killed it. A boar hog could be as tall as your waist and have tusks so long you could see them several hundred yards away. Hogs were to be avoided. Snakes you could go around and leave them in the dust, but you couldn't outrun a hog. Yes, bear and alligators were also somewhat of a worry. One day, we even saw some evidence of a bear. He'd been following my footprints, but I never heard or sighted it.

My first field day with Harry B. down near Townsend, Georgia, was most interesting. We were setting up a drainage study. There would be plots (tree measuring areas) measured on the ditch side of a drain field, that drained water away from the trees. The ditches actually drained a round pond. This allowed trees that normally grew in standing water to survive and thrive by draining away excess water. Later, we found that, during drought, the removal of round pond water produced more severe drought conditions. Round ponds actually purged the soil with much needed moisture during droughts.

Harry handed me a roll of white flagging tape and said to me, "Ken, go up there on that hill and flag off that ridge line so we know to which side rainwater will flow." I stopped dead in my tracks. The ground was flat as a fritter.

"What ridgeline Mr. B.?" I asked.

"Up there on top of that hill, see it? Just run down that ridge till you get to the ditch."

I was embarrassed. There was no ridge, hill or anything that looked like a hill. So, I squatted down and crept forward to where I thought there was a ridge and began running tape to the ditch. I figured a teeny tiny ridge spur ran like a big one, so I ran it pretty much straight to the ditch. He was happy.

Working down on this part of the Sapelo Forest behind Townsend, Georgia, there were a lot of wild pigs and domestic pigs. Once I saw a wild hog, black and huge. I could clearly see his tusks. I stopped dead in my tracks and backtracked carefully – never turning my back on him. I was glad to avoid that confrontation that day. On subsequent days, little teenage piglets – shoats is what they are called – started following me. The shoats kept their distance, but followed me to my truck. I was alone, so I used the time productively. I got my lunch, climbed up into the truck and began to eat. The shoats had congregated at the tail end of the truck, squealing and jostling for position, so I threw them my cheese crackers. This was a mistake, because every day I went down there to work, and I was alone, they would hear my truck and follow me all day long, waiting for lunch.

During the summer of 1976, we were tasked to look for pitch canker outbreaks throughout the southeastern land of Union Camp. From South Carolina to Florida, we drove every working circle road and mapped pitch canker trees. Florida had a huge break out of pitch canker, killing over approximately 100,000 trees (eventually up to 1,000 acres of dead trees). Our boss told us that he wanted quick results. We were to drive the roads, keep looking up, and mark on a compartment map every pitch canker dead top we saw with a red X and every tree oozing copious amounts of resin and dying from the top down. Make a red X at the location and put the number of Xs you think is the "intensity" of the kill at this location. This is called an empirical study, and there was no need to be super accurate except for the location.

So, armed with maps and red pencils, we began our survey. Two crews rode every road, trail, and woods-trail Union Camp owned. Marking the tree density of pitch canker, we discovered that some intersections had heavier concentrations of pitch canker. Around chicken coups and chicken farms, we found numerous trees oozing and dying from pitch canker. The survey took several weeks to complete.

Right after Christmas, Union Camp hired a scientist from Scandinavia to come and look at the pitch canker outbreak. He was a Ph.D. in tree diseases and considered an endemic disease tree expert. He had a meeting with us and asked our opinion about the outbreak. All of us gave him our honest assessment. We agreed that it was found heaviest around chicken farms. It was heavier around open areas than closed, tight areas, unless of course, you were in Florida, where entire tracts of land had died.

My counterpart, Joel M. and I mentioned we saw birds sitting in the tops of trees, everywhere, both in the infected areas and the uninfected areas. I told him I thought birds were the carriers and that they picked it up from chicken poop. Well, I got pretty much laughed out of the room. So, we technicians shrugged our shoulders and left. Outside, we complained that we had spent the most time looking at this stupid disease and we figured we had nailed it.

An hour later we were called back into the office. The doctor gave us our marching orders. Go kill some birds in the infected areas and bring their bodies to Rincon for analysis. The next day, with .22 high power rifles zeroed in, we loaded up two crews and headed to the infected areas. Each crew collected about six birds. Mostly crows, some robins, and other birds that were large in size. Using protective gloves, we put the birds in plastic bags and stored them in a cooler. We delivered the birds late that afternoon. I was surprised to see the Ph.D. was still in the office waiting on us. He took the birds with him, and we didn't see him again, but the report we saw was basically this:

Evidence has shown that birds are a carrier of the pitch canker virus. Additional evidence pointed at a relationship between chicken farms and pitch canker attacks on local pine trees. It is estimated that the fertilizer used to fertilize the trees in Florida, pure chicken waste nitrogen, contained the pitch canker in the nitrogen. When fertilized, the local birds went to the ground to eat the chicken droppings and then flew into tops of local trees, thus spreading the infection from the ground to the tree tops.

In essence, he wrote pretty much what we said had happened. We didn't receive any recognition from the company on our discovery, but then, that's corporate America. They would rather pay a PhD $100,000 to come over and give his opinion instead of listening to a bunch of dirty, tired, worn out forest rangers.

If this was just one case study of Union Camp hiring someone from out of state, or from another university, to come look at a problem instead of using their own force of technicians, I wouldn't be so boisterous about bringing these things up. But the company constantly did this.

Another time, a grand old tree in Savannah, known as the "Savannah Oak," was not doing well as it had "die back" in it. Union Camp was asked to look at the tree, but they hired a Ph.D. in hardwood studies to look at the tree and write his recommendation. This cost the company $50,000, and we technicians wondered why they were paying an outside consultant this much money to look at a tree.

So, one afternoon we swung through Savannah behind the old Candler Hospital on Abercorn Street. We drove behind the old hospital, which had been converted into a home for elderly people, and took a squint at the grand old Virginia Oak (Quercus Virginiana). With that one look, we knew exactly what had happened; we nailed the problem instantly.

There was no question someone had paved the parking lot all the way around the tree, 360 degrees, with asphalt leaving no air grates in the asphalt to allow the tree's roots to breathe. They were slowly suffocating the grand old tree due to their lack of understanding about tree roots. They have to breathe; they need water. The tips of the roots have a relationship with the soil, and if you choke out the roots, you kill the tree. Case solved. However, the Ph.D. came down and did his study then composed a report, made his 50k, and went home. What did he recommend? Yep, you got it, put in air grates so the tree roots could breathe. This lack of trust in using your own resources plagued the company until I left it in 1987.

CHAPTER 5

What Does a Forest Ranger Do Anyway?–1973

I once wrote a dissertation on the great outdoors and all those things that can bite, lick, suck, sting, scratch, poison, and just plain hurt you in the woods. Sometimes, the great outdoors wasn't so great, especially if you had to pick more than 80 ticks off your body every single day. No, the woods usually were a hot, sticky, muggy, breathtaking, sucky place

But the woods also had those rare moments, those snippets of life that would stick with you all the rest of your life.

While working for Union Camp, cutting brush lines was hard work. It allowed us to make sure we were inside the plots. The trees were measured with either a nail being driven into it at Diameter Breast Height (DBH) or given, on a map, the number of feet between trees to the next tree, and the diameter taken at DBH. Since all of us were trained in stepping off a chain (66 feet), finding the distance between trees was no problem.

Tree heights were difficult to estimate, but with practice, you got very good at seeing the tree top and getting its height with a Blume Leise or Haga altimeter. We then added to the measurements of tree height and DBH the condition of the tree, type of disease it had, and whether it had bug damage or some other damage. With the DBH and height, you could figure its basal area and how much it would grow in cords per acre per year. All of these measurements created math problems. We usually used an old-time computer to get the answers for our boss. We called it "the sum of the squares" when looking for the average diameter of the tree plot.

In 1977, I worked with Mr. M. on several seeding studies. The trees had been seeded by helicopter which, in my mind, was a bad idea. The trees in a quarter-acre plot or even a fifth-acre plot were so thick it would take several sheets of paper per plot to record the information. The trees were so crowded they looked like the hair on a dog's back, and when you measured a tree, your elbow sometimes banged into the tree beside you. This proved to be my undoing one day down on the Okefenokee forest, near the big swamp.

As we went through the seeded area, it was found that the ground was covered in sawtooth palmetto. These palmetto bushes tended to shred your pants and boot shoe laces. Normally we wore plastic snake leggings, but any jeans that stuck out below this were shredded to pieces. Once inside the seeded-in plantation, that was probably fifteen to twenty years old, the ground was bare of any vegetation because the trees had choked off all sunlight.

I was measuring along rather swiftly, calling off DBH while Joel was shooting heights, and Mr. M. was taking notes. I came to the next tree, threw the D tape around it, and pulled it tight, sticking my elbow into the adjacent tree. At this very spot, red wasps had built a huge nest, and, within seconds, I was repeatedly stung by a bevy of ticked-off wasps! That really hurt, and I dropped everything and ran. Luckily, I didn't receive another sting, but I had probably six welts and an elbow growing to the size of a softball. Yes, that hurt and slowed me down, but I continued to measure trees, including the wasp nest tree. Why not? I had already knocked the nest to the ground, the wasps were out being mad somewhere else.

We measured many fertilization plots where each tree had a nail with a number on it. Most plots had between 50 and 70 trees. Each tree was measured for DBH and height, diseases, and bugs, which are normal measurements for any research plot.

One day, we received a letter from our laboratory in Racine, Wisconsin. They were establishing fertilization plots in Wisconsin and wanted to know what type of special pencil did we use on the aluminum nail heads. Randy brought the letter outside to the group of us and we all got a good laugh out of their request. It was so innocent and sincere, yet we couldn't believe they didn't know what we used, or why. Randy wrote a nice handwritten note and packaged up a box of number 2 pencils and mailed them to Racine. I guess they didn't know the carbon interacts with the nail head and makes a permanent number that will not wash or rub off.

We poked fun at Racine because they were so easy to pick at – plus, they were Yankees. About every three months, we bundled up approximately six full-sized trees to ship to Racine for experiments in the amount of tars and oils they could extract. We found six southern pine trees of about 8" DBH and cut them down. While on the ground, we would lop off the tops at a 4" diameter. After we removed the limbs, we would take a square-nose shovel and remove all the bark. This is the way the old pioneers removed bark. They removed the bark so the tree would dry and last a lot longer in a log cabin than if the bark had been left on the log. Removing the bark helped Racine with extracting the oils and tars from each bole.

We cut up the tree in pulp wood length of 5 ¼ foot lengths and wrapped each tree in felt. Then, we tied it up with rope and took it to a local truck shipping company. All this was done in one day, usually right after lunch we would drop the load off to the trucking company. Racine would get the wood a day later and they would conduct their experiments.

Later that year, we received another letter from Racine. This time they specifically wanted to know how we cut down six trees, removed the bark so quickly, and shipped all of them in one day. They tried to conduct the same experiment in Wisconsin but failed to meet any of our timelines. As a matter of fact, they wanted to know how we had removed the bark so quickly. They cut down the trees, bucked them up into 5¼ foot-long pieces and then began to remove the bark with a putty knife. We were stunned. Randy went inside and explained how we did our bark removal; they didn't believe we used a square-nosed shovel and walked the entire length of the tree. I think after this, they kept their requests for additional methods to themselves. We never received another request, at least not one I'm familiar with.

In 1978, we planted 10,000 eucalyptus trees at Egypt, Georgia, and another 10,000 trees at Palmetto Bluff, South Carolina. Someone had the bright idea that Georgia and Brazil were about on the same parallel but in different hemispheres. Certainly, if eucalyptus grew in Brazil, it would grow in Georgia. This was during a dry summer and we had to water all 20,000 trees and add furadan to each tree. Furadan is a systemic insecticide and would kill any harmful bugs that attacked the tree. Each furadan drop, about 5 oz., had to be covered with a little dirt. We did this to 20,000 trees in about a day and a half. Not only did we water the trees, but we kept the weeds away from them. We hoed all 20,000 trees once a week.

By early fall, the mortality rate of the trees shot up, and by winter, almost 80% of the trees were dead. By the time the spring arrived, they'd all seemed to perish.

None survived the winter, even though Brazil and other South American countries have similar weather. Well, what was finally written up as the verdict on using eucalyptus trees in Georgia was it would be folly, a complete failure. The differences between Georgia's very cold mornings, and blistering hot afternoons killed the trees outright. They could not adapt to Georgia's great disparity between cold mornings and hot afternoons.

We went to Soil School in 1979, and I worked with Donnie B. in the field as a soil assistant. He was tasked to soil map all Union Camp land in the southeastern United States. This was a daunting task even for a soil scientist and an assistant. Eventually, they hired John K. from up north. He was a likeable guy but had to learn the south and the type terrain and bugs and whatnot the south throws at you.

One afternoon, we stopped into his Savannah office to pay a visit. John was out at another meeting. Since John was gone for the afternoon, Donnie B. and I decided to turn his office around 180 degrees. What was on the south wall was now on the north wall, and what was on the east wall was now on the west wall. This included his pictures. It didn't take long and we knew he would enjoy a different view.

Union Camp came up with a nice bumper sticker, *Grow Your Fair Share of Fresh Air – Plant Trees.* John had a brand new truck and when I told him I had an extra sticker for his bumper, he was adamant he wasn't going to booger up his truck with bumper stickers. Well, that was a challenge. I low-crawled around behind his truck, coming through the weeds, and placed the sticker square on the driver's side of his back bumper. He didn't notice that sticker for several months. When he accused me of putting it there, I denied it, but eventually, I owned up to it.

At Donnie's soil classes and soil reviews he taught, we would dig a ten-foot-wide by twelve-foot-long pit, at least 96" deep. We even cut a staircase set of earthen steps down into the bottom of the pit. Donnie would take his knife and flake off the sides of the soil and taking nails and string, he would identify different soil horizons. This was an impressive teaching tool, and although we usually worked hard at digging those training pits, we got to join in with the crowd and learn about soils ourselves. It was our reward for our hard work.

One summer, I was given a part-time summer worker to help me spray treetops that were lying about during a thinning operation. This was to keep the bug populations down. On our first day at work together, I took him to the Sapelo forest. It had rained and flooded the road and woods where the tops lay, but they needed to be sprayed. Once we arrived, I told him we were going to have to slog through knee-deep water to the upland where the tops lay. We sprayed them and finished our job in several hours, then slogged our way back out to the truck. He muttered under his breath that I was a crazy-ass Vietnam veteran. I just told him that getting your feet wet was part of the job. I suggested he put his boots in front of the bottom of his refrigerator to dry them out overnight. That's what I did. He was amused.

That very next day, we were near the Ogeechee River, just off of Georgia Highway 119. It was about 101degrees F. It was so hot and muggy you knew it was going to rain, but until then we had to suffer the heat. He was miserable, but he stuck it out. About the time we were going to quit, he said to me, "Ken, where is that train at?"

I said to him, "What train? There isn't a train anywhere near here."

"No, Ken, I hear a diesel engine train, where is it?" I looked at him, half expecting to see a boy dying of delirium, but instead, I saw him looking off into the woods and, from his waist to the ground, I couldn't see his body for the number of hornets that were encircling him.

I yelled, "Joe get out of there! Hornets!" He ran like he was an Olympic sprinter, opened the truck door, and slammed it shut. I walked out of the woods to the truck and put my sprayer up and spied that his was missing. "Joe, where's your sprayer?"

"I left it up there where the hornets are," he answered.

I asked him, "Joe, go pick up your sprayer."

He said, "No, they don't pay me enough to go pick up that sprayer."

In a way, I had to agree, he was scared and he probably would get killed by hornets, so I walked back into the woods, amongst the swarming hornets. I slowly bent down and picked up the sprayer and backed out of the swarm slowly. I returned to the truck and put the sprayer in the back.

I think he thought I was going to yell at him, but I didn't. I laughed and got him to laughing, and we both said that was probably the strangest thing either of us had ever experienced. After that day, he had a lot more respect for me, and I didn't work him to the point of exhaustion. He became a pretty good helper. I have forgotten his name, but his father was a CEO for one of the big bologna companies up north.

While there are so many stories I could tell, all of which are true, this next story, despite being a little crude, is very funny. Having said that, narcolepsy (the fainting/sleeping sickness) isn't a funny condition. It can cause some funny or harrowing events, but the people with the condition find it to be debilitating and hard to control.

One of my co-workers had narcolepsy, and if you told a joke and he started to laugh, he would faint. If we were planting trees and Randy told a dirty joke, we would all start laughing, but Jim would start to laugh and then faint. It wasn't funny, not at all. But every time he tried to get up, Randy would hit the punch line again and down he'd go for another few minutes. Now this was cruel, but Jim took it pretty well and he faced his condition head-on with medicine and discipline.

No one ever told a joke when Jim was driving. And when he was feeling good, he had pretty good control of the fainting spells. One April, Bob H. came down to measure his hardwood growth and yield plots. He had to get these measured before the leaves came out so you could get an accurate look at the tops for heights. Hardwoods grow slow and most of the plots were in swampy areas down around Richmond Hill, Georgia, and over near South Carolina Highway 278. These were very swampy and wet places that usually had two or three feet of water.

Bob was funny and had a great sense of humor, and it wasn't unlike any of us to tell a story or two. Randy was shooting heights, Joel was doing the target for the altimeter, Jim was taking notes, and I was doing DBHs and hunting the next numbered tree. Bob was loafing and watching; he was the boss. We had made great progress that day, measuring several hardwood plots and about to finish up, when Randy started a story about a Japanese forester named Fuzakizo that had once visited us. Now, Fuzakizo was into flowers.

He constantly stopped us doing our measurements on Growth and Yield plots to ask, "What flower this?"

Randy would answer, "That's Queen Ann's Lace."

"What flower this?"

Randy would answer. "Fuzakizo, that's a milk wort." In a way, it was very annoying but we tried to be nice hosts and answered all his questions.

Randy continued the story. "I had a bad stomach that morning, and when I jumped a little stream, I cut a real bad one, bad gas. Fuzakizo started to jump right behind me, but he stopped. He picked a yellow honeysuckle flower and he smelled it. He shook his head in a repugnant way and asked, "What is this?"

Randy said, "I answered him, saying 'it's a fart blossom.'"

Well needless to say, that triggered everyone into roars of laughter, and when I spied Jim, he was going down, in little quick jerks trying not to go underwater, but he did. I feared we might have drowned Jim as he went totally underwater, notes and all. We rushed to him and snatched him out of the water and held him up till he came to his senses. The notes were under two feet of water and were soaked. When I finally found the clipboard, Bob H. was not laughing. He was so mad at us for telling that story he made us quit for the day. Good thing because Jim was not in any shape to work.

Bob could have made trouble for us, but he himself was the victim of always messing something up. I understand that he had a big tour going on in the forests in Virginia and was rushing from site to site along a company road. He had forgotten about the rain they had during the night. Donnie always said if you spit in the Meherrin River, it floods. Bob, in his haste to get to the next plot, rounded the corner and drove his company car into the Meherrin River.

They recovered the car and got it back on the road, and Bob continued his research with hardwood trees. He asked for Randy, Joel, and me to help him with hardwood research plots in Alabama. We saved the easiest plots for last; those were the sweetgum plantations planted near the Prattville plant, in Prattville Alabama. The trees were planted in rows and were superior sweetgum trees (Liquidambar styraciflua). The tree heights were about 25 to 30 feet and had an average diameter at breast height (DBH) of about 5 to 7 inches. Some were bigger, some were smaller, but they appeared to be uniform in height and diameter.

While measuring the trees we were fighting off the smell of the paper-mill. We were quite a few feet below the mill, which was near the river. All of us complained of the smell and headaches it was causing, so we were in a hurry to get out of there and find some fresh air. We were about halfway done measuring when Bob decided he needed to sit down to rest while taking notes. Joel and I continued to measure trees. Now the note taker calls back the numbers as he writes it down to make double sure he has the correct figure. After about five trees, we noticed nothing but silence coming from Bob. I looked back and Bob was dead asleep leaning on a tree. We rushed back to him and sat down, waking him up.

"Bob! Wake up. Hey, wake up!" I said, shaking him by the shoulders.

He stared at me, glassy-eyed and said he was really tired. That's when Joel and I both yawned and, at the same time, said, "I'm tired too." We had the urge to just lay down for a rest, but all of us knew we were being starved for oxygen.

Bob decided that we should leave for the day and come back the next day and finish up. I honestly think we were very close to killing ourselves with some chemical that was settling down in the area next to the river. I'm not a chemist, but paper-mills use a lot of sulfur dioxide to wash the paper chips and break them down into lignin for making paper bags. The next day we checked wind conditions and the smell before going back and finishing the measurements.

There are a million snake stories, but the reader would die of boredom before I could write all of them down in this book. So here goes just one story, and then I will move on. Union Camp bought us brand new snake leggings called gator chaps. These chaps are worn over your boots and pants and protect you from both snakes and briars. The bottom portion is a flexible aluminum tube with a zipper up the back. The top portion is a very tough briar resistant chap that protects you from briars and brush.

It was common for equipment to be mixed between workers, so I took orange tree marking paint and sprayed a wide orange stripe up the side of my leggings, making them look awful, but they were still functional. Carey T. looked at those chaps and said, "Luikart, I'd be embarrassed to wear those things. I'd never put those on my body."

My retort was "Exactly."

On a trip to Florida, we took the Blazer and a truck. We had a large crew that was going to measure a very large stand of two-year-old trees. Diameters were taken at 6 inches above the ground level for small seedlings, so we took turns using the calipers and reaching down into the grass to measure the diameter. As we dressed, snakes were on our minds. This would be a good place to get snake bit.

We had Darrel G. with us, a new employee, and he had a brand new pair of gator chaps too. He was younger and eager to learn and show that he was a team player, so he hurried and grabbed the height measuring stick and rushed down the road. I saw him leap the ditch and go forward to a post to find out where the starting point was when we heard a loud THUNK and saw him fall backward onto the dirt road. He let out a scream, and we thought he was snake bit.

We rushed to him to quickly check him over. I looked at his aluminum snake legging and the snake had struck him mid-shinbone and had completely dented the aluminum in several inches. I was dumbfounded, that must have been a huge snake. We found out it was.

Jim S. dispatched the snake. Normally, we wouldn't kill a rattlesnake, however, it was in our way and in our plots, and it had to go. The snake's body was as big around as my upper thigh and its head was as wide as my hand. That was a big snake.

Darrell was petrified. No, he was terrified. There was no way of getting any work out of him after that, so we made him the keeper of the water jug while we measured the plots. Needless to say, each one of us that reached down to measure one of the thousands of seedlings that needed a measurement had that snake etched in our minds. Sometimes you just have to block things out and do your job, or you will never get anything done.

Forestry was my first love, way back in high school. I always knew that was the path I wanted to follow. But that path was fraught with problems I didn't even realize were affecting me. I was alive, I was successful, but I was not fully inside of my body. Something had left me, and left me hollow. This was a struggle that is difficult to explain.

CHAPTER 6

The Dark Days–1975

I started with Union Camp in 1973. I left the Army in January, 1971, and graduated from Lake City Forest Ranger School in August 1973. While going to Ranger School, I had several episodes that should have revealed my need for help coping with PTSD (Post Traumatic Stress Disorder).

At that time, I didn't like crowds or being around a lot of people when I went shopping with Sandi. I didn't trust anyone and warily kept my eyes on people. I didn't like eating in restaurants, and always, *always* took the seat where I could watch the main entrance. I didn't like braggarts or loud-mouthed people. I didn't like people shouting around me, or even talking loudly to me. Also, sirens, lightning, brooms falling and hitting the floor, cars backfiring, and other sudden, loud sounds would send me to the ground. These were automatic knee-jerk reactions I couldn't help.

One night, after moving to Boyd's trailer park in Rincon, a train roared through town and sounded its horn; it was extremely noisy. Sandi, thinking it was a tornado, rolled out of bed to the right and attempted to pull the top mattress over her. Unfortunately, she couldn't budge the mattress because I yelled, "Incoming" as I rolled out of bed to the left, throwing the dog and the cat into the air, all the while trying to pull the mattress over me. We were canceling each other out on the mattress deal until finally, we both realized it was just a train.

There were many nights I would stay up late at night, feeling that something just wasn't right. One night in Lake City, I woke up and spied the night light above our dresser in our house trailer. I came up out of bed with fist drawn back, ready to break a window out to smash the intruder in the face. Thankfully, Sandi caught my arm.

I wasn't aware of PTSD, or Traumatic Brain Injury (TBI) that soldiers are regularly treated for today. While in Vietnam, I was exposed to hundreds of rounds of rockets and mortars and outgoing artillery fire from 8" and 175mm guns. During that time, I had been knocked down at least three times from close calls, one of which was just yards from me. Those shock waves and that experience, plus the trauma of losing men just down the road to friendly artillery fire from the 18th ARVN Division, played havoc with my mind.

One afternoon, I was sitting in the outside shop's bathroom at Union Camp, when my mind went blank. I wasn't sure where I was, and I felt as though my inner self was missing. There was no response to mental inquiries. I was unable to express or even internally feel any feelings; I had no regrets, no happiness or sadness. I had emotionally detached. As I sat there in a stupor, I wondered what I was doing, who I was, and where I was. I went into the breakroom and sat there for a little while, trying to get my mind to focus. But my little conscious voice was gone. It just wasn't there, and I did not know what was wrong with me.

I went into deep depression and had frequent bouts of moodiness. It felt like I had just run out of steam. When you work in the woods, this is terrible because you have to pull your weight. In the woods there was no one to talk to, no one to turn to.

April of 1975 rolled around and our nation did nothing to help when Vietnam fell into communist hands. This added even more depression to my already troubled mind. I went to see Doctor R. in Rincon. He treated me for depression and got me on anti-depressants. No one at work knew this, or probably even cared, so, I kept it to myself.

When working in the woods, lightning strikes would force me to the ground, amid much laughter and joking among my colleagues as they made fun of me. I would just stay low for a minute or two and then get back up and brush myself off. They saw the moodiness and the fear of loud noises, those things I couldn't hide.

In September of 1975, I stopped a jeep load of artillerymen in Springfield. We talked through the window and I asked them if they were taking men into the

Springfield unit. Their officer said "Sure, what rank are you? And what's your MOS?"

I said "I'm a 96B20 Intel Analyst, and a Spec 5."

He was quiet for a moment. "Then you can read a map, right?"

I responded "Yes Sir, I read maps pretty darn good."

He came back at me quickly. "Well, we can take you in the unit, drop you a rank, and make you a forward observer." *Blink blink.* I was stunned. The forward observer thing wasn't such a good deal, but dropping me a rank?

No way. I said "Thanks, I'll think about it." I never thought about it again.

In September 1975, I went by the Georgia Air Guard's 165th Tactical Airlift Group, which was based, and still is, at Savannah Airport. Mike B. talked with me and I joined the Air Guard as an Intelligence NCO, kept my Spec 5 rank, and went to work with then Captain Ed W. He was a brand new Intel Officer and I was replacing an Intel NCO that was leaving. That was how I ended up staying another thirty-three years with the Air National Guard.

Needless to say, I was able to right myself from the depression and got off the medication. I still had some PTSD problems but getting back into the military, getting back into studying enemy combat units, surface to air missiles, antiaircraft fire, and aircraft helped me shake off the deep pangs of PTSD as long as I was busy working military problems again.

I wrote several training syllabuses on Soviet chemical, biological, and nuclear weapons doctrine. I also wrote a syllabus for identification of Soviet, French, and US aircraft. At that time, they were the primary countries producing aircraft. I also wrote a training class on Surface to Air Missiles.

In those days, the 1970s, it was "death by vu-graph." You had to make vu-graphs the hard way using a special printer that imprinted a picture onto a plastic 8" x 11" stock, then taped it into a paper vu-graph frame. We also used the slide projector and movies to enhance training.

I had very little resistance when training aircrews when I first arrived. We had an abundance of Vietnam C-130 pilots and they listened intently and respected my background. As time moved forward and those men retired, it became harder to convince younger pilots that the threat of dying in a combat situation, was real. However, newer protective systems were being developed for the C-130.

Those systems were developed because of the efforts of many veteran intelligence officers and their newly formed tactics officers. Major Harry Weir, from West Virginia's Air National Guard, wrote a manual for flying the C-130 aircraft in a threat environment. The Air Force was disgusted and irritated over this document and ordered all copies to be destroyed. Just about every intelligence office I knew ignored this order and kept the book, classified secret, in their training material as "reference material."

In May of 1979, I was commissioned as an Air Intelligence Officer. I received a direct commission from Technical Sergeant (E-6), to 1st Lieutenant. I took the position as the part time officer assigned to the Intel Section. Every year, the C-130 Intel and Tactics Officers and NCO's attended the conferences. On many subsequent Intelligence conferences we kept hitting our leadership on producing our own MCM 3-1, the Air Force's official document on flying the C-130 in combat. One thing that hastened this was missions into El Salvador and threats from the SA-7 surface to air missile.

Since El Salvador was a war zone, and killing on both sides was rampant, landing at their airfields required going back to Vietnam-type tactics. In addition, West Virginia and other Air Guard units, mounted three flare guns on a bar that was attached to the open parachute entrance to the aircraft. Upon final descent, the flare guns would be fired to ward off any possible surface-to-air heat-seeking missile. Needless to say, there were repercussions regarding this novel idea. Setting the woods on fire, or someone's house, brought complaints. I think this hastened the development of C-130 defensive systems.

Everyone has seen the flying "Angel" when a C-130 fires all of its flares at once. This provided on-board capabilities to defeat hand held surface to air missiles. In addition, Rosecrans Air National Guard Base at St. Joe, Missouri, became the home of the C-130 flying tactics school. An intelligence officer assigned to the flying tactics school would dress up like a Soviet officer and parade out on the stage. He was presented as a guest speaker to all the attendees, and his dress and appearance was that of a Bolshevik.

He would strut onto the stage and spend nearly thirty minutes berating the United States, its military, and the weak and simple-minded American C-130 pilots. He had the audience so mad that they were yelling at him, calling him names and threatening him. Finally, when he saw he had them totally fooled, he broke into his English and took off his blouse to show them he was St. Joe's Intelligence Officer. This had been his way of introducing the aircrews to Soviet thought.

After training at St. Joe, the aircraft and crews went to Tucson, Arizona. They flew the Tonopah range, over southern Arizona. Eventually this training was tempered by flying combat exercises out of Nellis Air Force Base. This schooling was the best in the Air Force. Intelligence Officers attended the CAT School (Combat Aircrew Training School). We learned how to use the C-130 tactics in every day missions, especially into hostile territory.

Lieutenant Colonel Vanita S. took Colonel W.'s place as the director of intel in 1979. She came over from working intelligence supporting Search and Rescue missions for downed aircrew in Vietnam. She worked Intel for the crewmember of BAT-21. (Bat 21 –Wikipedia)

The following is a story of Lt. Colonel Hambleton, a navigator on an EB-66 (Electronic Warfare Aircraft used to jam enemy radar) that was shot down on Easter Sunday in 1972. By using his radio combined with his avid love of golf, he escaped from enemy territory using various golf courses. By using the direction and distances from the tee to the green, he was able to escape to friendly forces. Vanita played a role in that recovery and came to our unit highly recommended.

In the 1980s, it was unusual to see many female majors or lieutenant colonels in the Air Force. Lieutenant Colonel Vanita S. was not a tall person however, she had the temperament of a trapped rattlesnake. I once observed how she handled the persistent needling and nitpicking from a Lieutenant Administrative Inspector from the Inspector General's team. After several minutes of pointing out to us printing errors in our documents from Defense Intelligence Agency, she got up, went directly to the safe, snatched the file folders out of the Lieutenant's hands, put them back in the safe, slammed the safe drawer closed and spun the dial locking the safe, all in one move. Her only comment was, "The Admin Inspection of our safes is over. You're excused." She kicked him out of the room. I was impressed.

In 1987, Vanita wanted to move closer to home, so she transferred to a unit in Michigan. That left a vacancy in the office whereupon I was able to apply for the job and received it. Geoclyn W., a principle from

Georgia's Richmond County schools, was chosen as the second officer in the Intel section. Geoclyn was the first black female officer chosen in the Georgia Air National Guard. This was in 1987.

On a mission to El Salvador in the late 1980s, the C-130 I was on hit a light pole. On taxiing to the runway, following the lines painted on the tarmac, the aircraft commander swung around to line up on the runway. When he did, the left wing of the aircraft struck a light-pole. We all felt the *bump* but we couldn't see what debris we assumed we'd run over. Finally, the pilot noticed the light pole driven two feet into the left outside wing. At that point, fuel was pouring out and gushing onto the taxiway. The pilot pulled the alarm and everyone exited the aircraft, running out the rear, as instructed in our safety briefing. We gathered up behind the aircraft whereupon I grabbed a fire extinguisher on wheels. I took one step toward the aircraft and stopped. Fuel was ankle-deep on the taxiway.

Our very experienced flight engineer cut all power to everything as the engines were being shut down. We noticed the aircraft tipping to the right as the left wing emptied its fuel. Finally, the right wing touched the ground and there sat our ride, a wounded bird. The fire department rushed out and began diluting the fuel. The fire chief ordered our Flight Engineer to go "inside the aircraft and move the fuel from the right side to the left side in order to "right" the aircraft. I remember his remark to the fireman, "No way in hell I'm going back into that aircraft and turn on an electrical system!" So, the fuel was pumped out of the right wing the old way and we were ushered to the infirmary to urinate into a cup.

Whenever there is an aircraft accident, everyone must take a drug and alcohol test. Blood is drawn and you must pee into a cup. This took some time; meanwhile, all of our belongings were still left on the aircraft where we had stowed them. When exiting an aircraft in an emergency, you don't stop to pick up anything.

After a lengthy health examination, we were standing outside of the infirmary. Colonel Rusty, our pilot, was standing outside and none of us had a hat on our heads. A full bird Colonel came sauntering by and remarked, "Colonel, where is your hat?"

Rusty replied, "Sir, I just wrecked a thirty-million dollar aircraft, and I don't care where my hat is!"

The Colonel blinked for a second and said, "Well, if I'd crashed a 30 million dollar aircraft, I wouldn't care where my hat was either." That was all that was said.

What saved the crew was everyone was clean, and they had all read the NOTAMs (Notices to Airmen). Those are notional things that should be read before you leave Operations to take off. The taxiway had just received new pavement and the lines painted on the taxiway were new. The problem was the lines were painted to fit fighter aircraft, not transports. There was nothing in the NOTAMs that spoke of any of this.

I won't bore you with all the three engine landings I've been a part of, one in New Hampshire and several at home at the Savannah Hilton Head International Airport. All I can say is I flew with the best transport crews in the military. Those men were Air Guardsmen, but were proficient and knew the C-130 systems from top to bottom. I would listen to the crew grill each other for hours on "what ifs." It made me feel safe that these men always had their heads into their mission.

Thirty-three years of duty with a C-130 unit meant occasionally experiencing bizarre occurrences. Duty to Panama, when Noriega was dictator, was hazardous because you had to go off base to other locations to eat, play golf, or visit a beach. Going off base was hazardous. Panamanian drivers' licenses were licenses to kill. We considered such duty extremely hazardous.

In downtown Panama City, just across the Bridge of Americas, was a school zone. In this school zone stood a cardboard man, six feet tall, holding up the "Alto" or *Stop* sign. A crew from our unit, who will not be named, had to go through this school zone. They were driving a blue sedan and stopped and grabbed up the cardboard man and stuffed him into the trunk. He was spirited back to Operations to be flown back to Georgia.

Sitting across the road from this little cardboard man and the school zone was the Balboa police station. They followed the car to Howard Air Force Base (AFB) and knew it was airmen that had taken the object. They called Howard and filed a complaint and the little policeman was returned to its rightful owners. The aircrew were threatened back at the 165th Airlift Wing by our commander. They were yelled at, but I do not think anyone was officially reprimanded.

While at Howard Air Force Base, the officers were required to walk downhill from the officer's barracks to their work centers. Of course, we also had to walk back up the hill. It was a pleasant walk, passing many of the two-story homes built during World War II. Each house was decorated, and there were toys in some yards. Other yards were manicured and had little trinkets placed here and there. One such yard had a wooden cow, just a simple little black and white wooden cow placed in front of the flowers. This is how the "wooden cow incident" occurred.

Some crew members walking by the little cow, painted all white with black spots, became fond of it. So they picked it up and took it to the BOQ (Barracks Officers Quarters.) and placed it on top of a blue sedan. They picked up some fruit from a nearby tree, decorating the back of the cow and trunk of the car as though the cow pooped on it. The Provost Marshal called the Commander of our task force, a navigator, and exclaimed, "Some of your aircrew are stealing a wooden cow from so and so's yard! I want that investigated." This cow, with some help from crew members, wandered all over the base.

Our Commander at the time, a Tactics Officer, replied, "Does the cow have a leash on it? Is it roaming freely?" I'm not sure I can repeat what was said between the two, however, that very afternoon, as we climbed the hill to our rooms, we passed the cow. We noticed a hole had been drilled into the bottom of its belly and a chain with a padlock went through the hole and was attached to a manhole cover. The cow was securely fastened so it would stay home and wouldn't end up roaming Howard Air Force Base.

At about the same time, we had an air incident at Rio Hato, the location of one of Noriega's houses. In the late 1980s around 1988, the Panamanians put 20mm antiaircraft guns around strategic locations. There also was an airfield near Rio Hato. This is where the battle of Rio Hato took place in 1989. Three of our aircraft on a training mission in 1988 were put in a holding pattern and told to circle prior to landing at Howard. The three aircraft burned holes in the sky, flying over boats, jungle, and water, looking at everything on the ground.

On one of their turns, the mission commander, a Vietnam veteran, saw Noriega's huge home and widened his circle to fly near the house. The Panamanians on the ground were excited that the aircraft broke into a no-fly zone. It is probably a miracle that the antiaircraft guns on the ground didn't shoot at them. Once the planes were allowed to land, the mission commander and pilots were in hot water and had to write a deposition concerning what happened and why they flew so close to Noriega's home.

Boredom and booze created some tough times for the mission commanders in Panama. Crew members of the *Animal House*, or barracks, were always into something unusual or semi destructive. On one episode, the commander had two naked men run past him, wearing nothing but hats. He threw his hands up in the air and walked back inside his room.

Another game the troops played was "How quick can the family of coati – a raccoon type animal with a prehensile tail – eat a fifty-pound bag of dog food. Some picked fifteen minutes, some an hour or two, one colonel picked twenty-four hours. He won. His reasoning was based on the size of their stomach and the amount of food in the dog food bag. He knew it would be at least a day, and he was right.

On December 20, 1989, the United States invaded Panama and arrested Noriega, their despot leader. Prior to this date, around 1988, our unit went to Panama for two weeks. This was a yearly rotation where Air Guard C-130 units would rotate in for two weeks at a time. They would marry up with a unit that was on their second week, so there were always two units of C130s in Panama at any given time. We were assigned to the Southern Command.

This was a very scary time in Panama. I had asked about a supposed ground attack between the Marines and monkeys near Howard AFB. I was told to mind my own business. If the government says the Marines were in a thirty-minute firefight with apes, it was with apes. I rolled my eyes.

While we were there, the Panamanian Defense Force erected numerous 20mm and 23mm antiaircraft guns at checkpoints, and road intersections, and around Howard AFB. I was there with three other intelligence officers and a non commissioned officer. We decided to take a tour of the city and check out gun locations.

We tried to see how close we could get to Noriega's house on an island southwest of Howard. We were doing okay until we came around a blind curve, and there was a huge roadblock with heavy machine guns and numerous guards. We stopped some 100 yards from their position. We started to turn around. I yelled, "Don't look at them! Don't look at them, don't look back, just go." We turned in the middle of the road, never looking back just went back the way we came around the corner, where we all drew a big sigh of relief.

In the 1990s, on a deployment to Germany, we were flying daily missions into Sarajevo, Bosnia Herzegovina. After we landed and taxied into position, we began unloading French soldiers and equipment. This took about fifteen minutes to complete, so engines were never shut off, just in case the airfield came under attack.

I was sitting up front beside the flight engineer when there was a *boom, boom, boom.* Smoke was rising from the far end of the runway, near the ruins of a small village. The flight engineer exclaimed through the intercom, "What was that?"

I said, in a calm voice, "That is a mortar attack."

"Are they shooting at us?" The crew was wondering what would come next.

I said, "No, if they wanted to hit us, we would be burning already, that's a mortar, and it's pretty accurate." The crew became believers in paying attention to the Intel briefings.

Both of my children, Jamey and Jennifer, were born during my time with the Air National Guard. I was the first Luikart in forty years to have a daughter born into the Luikart family or at least my immediate family. And since then my brother David has had a granddaughter that is turning into a beautiful young lady, her name is Molly. Your children are all you leave on this earth that is your legacy.

CHAPTER 7

The Seeds of a Legacy–1976

A recent magazine article claims that your children are not your legacy; you are your own legacy. I have often heard that the only things you leave behind on earth that are your legacy is your children – not your wealth, buildings, or libraries named after you, or streets that sport your name, but your children. So, I agree with the premise that your children are all you leave behind. They will carry on in this world. How you raise them and equip them for life is your legacy.

While you're raising your children, you are planting the seeds of a legacy, your legacy. Your children will grow up as you raise them; they will reflect your values. Raise them without respect or love, and they will show little respect or love for their fellow humans. Children are a parents' mirror. That old saying is true, I believe. Children reflect a parent, and so if you are a mean and horrible man to your wife, your children will grow up mean and horrible to their wives. Yes, there are exceptions to every rule, but we all know that, for the most part, it's a truism.

When Jamey was born in 1976, natural childbirth was a new type of birth experience during that period. We attended classes and learned all the tricks. The dutiful husband would be his wife's coach, aptly named because he did all the directing and yelling and helping, while the wife did all the work and endured all the pain. We were told when and how to use towels, paper bags, and lollipops. All these tools helped with distraction, or breathing or bolstering up a part that needs some pain relief. With all these tools in hand, theoretically, the husband was the most important part of the experience. I agreed to help and be a coach and was fully committed to helping Sandi endure her labor.

Sandi started labor early in the morning, and we rushed to the hospital for our natural childbirth experience. Loaded down with paper bags, towels, pillows, lollipops, and a husband, we were rolled toward the birthing room. Immediately, nurses began taking things away from Sandi. "You won't need pillows or towels, honey," they said.

Another nurse took away our lollipops, and yet another nurse said to me, "Only females go in here, sweetie, you need to wait in the father's waiting room." We objected and explained that we were having natural childbirth, but we didn't get our props, or the husband back, until the doctor came in and said it was okay. The problem was we were the first couple to have gone to that hospital to have a natural childbirth.

Several neighbors and relatives began to arrive and were waiting patiently for this happy event. The hours rolled by, and Sandi didn't dilate enough for birth. I did my best with pillows, bags, and coaching. By observing a monitor, I could tell when her next labor pain was coming before she knew it. I wasn't sure if my telling her it was coming was helping or hurting the situation. By lunchtime, we were exhausted, but we were still trying. Sandi's Aunt Jane commented to me, "I knew Sandi was in trouble when I saw a nurse reading a paperback book on the Lamaze method of childbirth."

That night they let Sandi sleep as best she could. The next morning as hour 32 rolled around, Sandi was a complete wreck. The doctor finally told Sandi she was going to need a C-section because she wasn't going to dilate enough for the head to pass through, and the baby was stressing. In spite of all our hard work, pillows, bags, lollipops, and husband were taken to the waiting room. I sat quietly and worried about Sandi. But shortly, the doctor came out and said I had a healthy baby boy, and Sandi was doing fine. I got to see my firstborn through the glass until I had dressed in a gown and mask. He was a perfect little boy. Harry Benjamin Luikart had joined our family.

My children were born during my worst years with PTSD. Jamey, especially, suffered under a strict disciplinarian father. As a military man, I expected him to be perfect, and of course, he was not. He was a boy trying to grow up in a protected environment.

Jamey was born in February, 1976, an election year, and the election for president was held that November. On Election Day, Sandi was going over to the Rincon Community Center to vote. Rincon was a much smaller town back then and the voting for most of Rincon was conducted in the Hinley building, a combined volunteer fire station and meeting hall.

Georgia Highway 21 was as old as George Washington and the Bartram Trail. It was the main route that the left wing of General Sherman's Army marched on towards Savannah. Sandi parked her car on the highway in a parking space adjacent to Georgia Highway 21. She exited the car with Jamey wrapped up in a blanket because it was chilly that afternoon. Jamey was not quite nine months old, so she cradled him carefully as she walked down the uneven and broken sidewalk in front of the building. Suddenly, the heel of her shoe caught in one of the jagged pieces of concrete in front of the building and caused her to pitch forward and fall on the cement. She was unable to put her hands out to break her fall as she clutched Jamey tightly and hit the cement with a thud. She tried to soften the fall for Jamey, but his head hit the cement.

Horrified, and hurting, because her elbow took most of the blow, she grabbed him up and rushed to Doctor R.'s office, just a few blocks away. Upon a quick examination, the doctor told her to take him to Effingham Hospital. There, they x-rayed his head and found nothing unusual and told her to take him back home, but watch him carefully. She left the hospital and returned to our trailer in Boyd's trailer park. Alone and scared, she watched and kept hovering over him for less than an hour before she saw very bad signs of a baby with a terrible head injury. She called the doctor's office and was told to bring him back in immediately.

I was working on the Research Forest planting progeny test trees. That was off of McCall road, on a woods road named Tower Road, just before the railroad track on the right side of the dirt road. We had radios back then and my radio call sign was "143." I heard the radio blare out "143 from Rincon." It was Mrs. C, the Research Forest secretary.

I answered, "143, go ahead."

"You need to go to Doctor R.'s office and meet your wife; your son has been hurt." That's all she would tell me, I asked to borrow one of the trucks and I raced back to Doctor R.'s office on Highway 21.

I went inside and the nurse said, "Out back, they're loading him up now–" She cut off her words and just pointed the direction.

Loading him up? What on earth? I thought. I stepped out back. Sandi was crying and she waved me into the back of the ambulance.

Earlier that afternoon, returning home from the hospital, Sandi noticed something unusual with Jamey. He would seem to go into a deep sleep, but for just a few minutes, then he'd wake up screaming and crying. She called Doctor R., who said to bring him right in. Upon seeing him for the second time, he immediately called Memorial Hospital and asked that a neurosurgeon meet the ambulance at the door. He told them it was urgent. The ride to the hospital took twenty minutes, an almost impossible feat as it was rush hour. Doctor R. told the ambulance attendant, James E., not to let Jamey's head move. This wonderful EMT placed sandbags on either side of Jamey's head. He then rode to Savannah, holding the sandbags in place with his knees.

At the hospital, we were met by Doctor D., who ordered an immediate CAT scan of his head, along with other quick tests. He came back a few minutes later and showed us a picture of Jamey's skull. I was horrified and scared. The picture showed a fractured skull and a huge blood clot in his head that had pressed his brain into only a third of his skull's space. It was more terrible than I can describe. Two-thirds of his skull was filled with blood.

I was sick. Sandi was mortified. But the scare didn't end with a picture, Doctor D. told us point blank, "I can try to save his life, but he only has a 30% chance of survival, and if he survives, he may well be a vegetable." That news almost caused me to faint.

Doctor D. turned and disappeared, Sandi was comforted by neighbors and family, I disappeared and found the chapel. I was alone when I entered. And here is where many people may disagree with me. Most Christians would say you cannot make a deal with God, that it doesn't work that way, you pray and leave it in God's hands *because God doesn't cut deals*.

I stood there a broken man, completely and utterly destroyed inside. I wore dirty work clothes, my wife was near hysterical, the doctor had no good news. And my firstborn son might not live.

I was lost.

At the altar, I fell to my knees. The chapel was quiet and softly lit, allowing a feeling of godliness. On my knees, I began to pray in earnest. Bent over at the altar, I prayed for my son. I loved Jamey, he was my pride and joy. He had just learned to walk. I'd taught him, at nine months, to play with his cars and blocks. He was so cute, we loved him so much. Now he was fighting for his life with only a 30% chance of surviving the operation. Thirty-percent of surviving are some lousy odds. Then, if he survived the surgery, he might still be left without most of his brain function.

I prayed, asking God to save my son. I told Him how Jamey was worthy of saving and there was something he was destined to be. Then I cut the deal. If you give me my son back, I promise You I will give back to you. I promise, I'll find something to give back to you that you will find worthy.

Meanwhile, the Rincon United Methodist Church had a prayer circle, by phone, asking each member to pray for my son. The pastor passed on the information about Jamey's condition and operation. Each member who was called prayed and called other members. I was not alone. My prayers were not in vain. Other people were praying with me. There is power in prayer.

I believe that sometimes you are given a second chance – and sometimes you are not. That's from the book of Job. The devil causes mayhem, death, destruction, war, and famine. Yes, all the bad things on earth are brought about by the devil. He is powerful, but Jesus is Omnipotent. He is greater than what we physically see in the universe.

After a short while, I raised my head. Tears streaked my face. I had cried like an inconsolable baby. I tried to dry my eyes and blow my nose in an effort to make myself more presentable to the small support crowd in the waiting room. I had made my promise, but I wasn't sure God would answer my prayer. The wait during the surgery was the longest two or three hours in my life. Finally, Doctor D. came out to see us, still wearing his scrubs. He explained what he found.

The fractured skull had caused interior bleeding. Had Jamey's scalp ruptured and the skull bled outward, he wouldn't have had such a large blood clot. Head wounds bleed quite heavily. Dr. D. had to open the skull, making a square with a "flap." Raising the flap, they drained the blood clot, thereby relieving the pressure put on the brain. Dr. D. noticed that Jamey had one lucky thing in his favor. The sack that the brain sits in, inside the skull, *was not ruptured.* That meant that the brain itself was not contaminated with external bacteria.

Jamey was sewed up and put in infant intensive care. We got to peek at him briefly and then were asked to step into the waiting room until he was fully awake the next morning. That night, from about 9:00 P.M. to morning was the longest night of our lives. Sandi and I had each other, our friends, our church, everyone was praying for Jamey. Everyone prayed just for him, for his recovery, not just from the operation, but from brain damage.

Early the next morning, just as the sun came up, we were called back to Jamey's room. When I walked in, I was stunned, absolutely just blown away! Jamey was standing in his crib, reaching out for us, crying for his bottle! He had tubes in his head, in his nose, and in his mouth. Honestly, he looked like an alien. But, he was hungry, crying for milk, and wanted to be fed.

Sandi asked the nurse for a bottle and she refused. I asked a second time, and she started to refuse me and I told her to find out if he can have a bottle or I'm unplugging him and taking him home. Frankly, I thought I was going to jail, but she called the surgeon who approved a little milk if Jamey could drink it.

He spent several more nights at the hospital, but soon was able to come home. He had lost the ability to walk, but we started working with him. His eye was knocked sideways, and his vision was impaired, but soon that cleared up. As he grew up, we looked for signs, but he soon began to fully recover. He regained his ability to walk, and talk, and grew up to have his own son, Nathan.

Jamey was an Eagle Scout, a Silver Congressional Medal recipient, a member of the Brotherhood Order of the Arrow, and he graduated from high school with honors. He went on to graduate from Georgia Southern University and works in insurance handling claims for Medicaid and Medicare. He's smart as a tack and has that wry Luikart sense of humor. Thanks be to God!

Jamey doesn't like for me to tell his story, but it's true. He was truly in a fight for his life, and at such a young age. He had the grit and toughness to survive, and Sandi and I had the support and love given us to survive. We had many people to thank in our church family for Jamey's life. As for my deal with God, a busy, omnipotent Creator, the Maker of heaven and earth, how was I going to give back?

I began later that winter as I tossed a football with two little boys in my backyard, Robbie and Jeff H. Robbie asked me if I'd be interested in helping his daddy with Boy Scouts. I said, "Yes."

I filled out paperwork to become an Assistant Scoutmaster, and was interviewed by the Scouting executive. By that time, we had sold our trailer and moved in with Sandi's mom and dad on West Johnson Street. Sandi's parents moved to Rincon from Dunedin, Florida, to be closer to their only grandchild after his accident.

Robert H. and I received almost thirty Webelos and regular scouts into Troop 665 in November 1977, exactly one year after Jamey's surgery. I had found something to give back to the Lord. I enjoyed Scouting and being fairly new to getting out of the US Army, was able to keep the discipline and make the Scouts line up, be quiet, and pay attention. Two weeks later, on the way home from a Scout meeting, Robert asked me a question. "Ken would you trade places with me? I mean, would you be the Scoutmaster and let me be the assistant?"

"Well, I need to ask Sandi, but I probably can do that." Sandi was mad at me. I had overextended my commitment, had made it more important in my life than normal for us. But, she relented and I became the Scoutmaster of Troop 665 in November or December of 1977. It's a commitment I kept until I was injured seriously in 2013, and became the troop's committee chairman.

As of this writing, it's the year 2020 and I'm a committee member of Troop 665B and also the Committee Chairman of Troop 665G, an all-girl BSA Troop. One troop meets on Monday night and the other on Tuesday night. Troop 665G is brand new and has borrowed some tents and gear to become a functional troop that camps, ties knots, and learns to cook on open fires, just like the boys. No, we are not coed; each troop is its own unit with different meeting nights.

I've been an active member and supporter of Scouts since 1977. I believe in what we teach as well as our agenda. In December 2019, a former Scout's father, Mr. Charley C., gave me a call and thanked me for training his son in first aid. Here's the story.

Thomas C., an adult who is an Eagle Scout, was working at his job in South Carolina as a supervisor. As the new supervisor at a fence company, he was responsible for making sure everything was on the truck before departing to the worksite. Nearby, in the shop, a workman was working a cross-cut saw when his sleeve got caught. The saw chewed into his hand and up his arm before it could be stopped.

Men in the plant hollered that someone was hurt bad and bleeding. Thomas ran and picked up the Stop Bleeding kit his company bought for such emergencies. Thomas assessed the situation quickly and applied a tourniquet at the proper distance above the cut artery. He applied dressings and kept applying dressings until he stopped the bleeding. Meanwhile, someone called 911, and the EMTs were on the way. Thomas finished bandaging the man and wrote down the time the tourniquet had been applied for the EMTs and hospital.

When the EMTs arrived, they inspected the medical work Thomas had applied and asked, "Who did this?" Everyone pointed at Thomas.

Thomas said, "I did. I knew where the Stop Bleeding kit was located and did what needed to be done."

The EMT looked at Thomas and said, "We're ready to transport, you've already done an excellent job. We don't have anything else to do here." They loaded him up and took him to the ambulance. But before they left for the hospital, the EMT asked Thomas, "Where did you learn all this?"

Thomas said, "From my Scoutmaster and our Troop first-aid practices."

The EMT smiled and said, "Well, he taught you well."

Ken and Sandi
Dunedin, FL
1971

Sandi
1969

Jamey and Jenny
1981

Jamey
1976

Jamey
1978

Jamey
1981

Jamey
1991

Jamey
Eagle Scout
1992

Jamey
High School Graduation
1994

Jamey
2013

Jamey and Amanda
2013

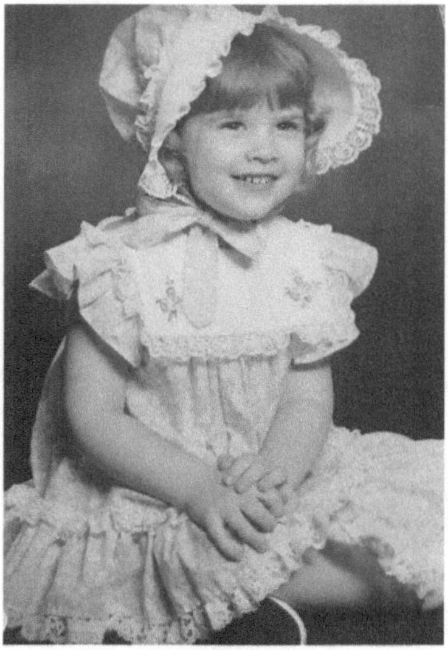

Jenny
1983

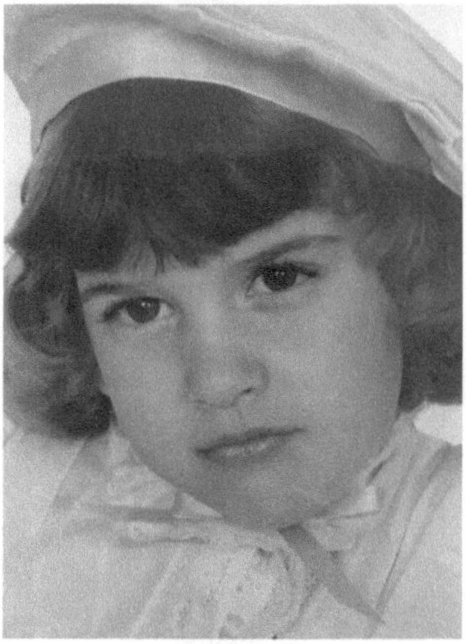

Jenny
1985

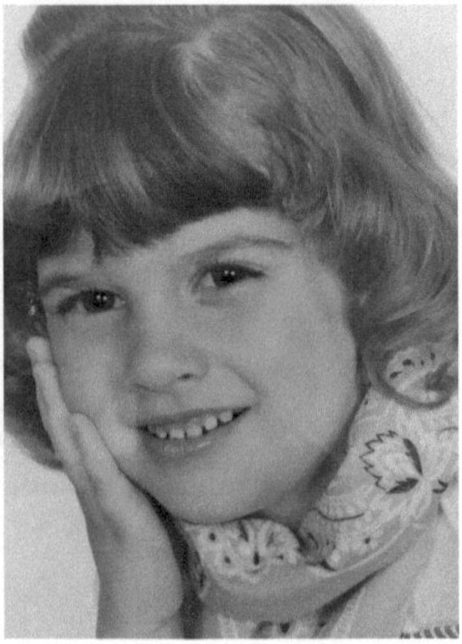

Jenny
1985

Jenny
First Saturday on River Street
Savannah, Ga.
1991

Jenny
Dance Recital
1996

Jenny
High School Graduation
1999

Jenny and Matt
2007

Jenny, Matt, Roman and Alex
2014

Jamey and Jenny
1998

Nathan, Alex, and Roman
Christmas
2017

Roman
2011

Roman
2013

Roman
First Day of Kindergarten
2016

Roman
Cub Scout District Pinewood Derby
2020

Alex
Christmas
2015

Alex
4 Year Pre-K Graduation
2019

Alex
Monkey Bridge
2019

Alex
2020

Alex and Roman
2014

Roman and Alex
2015

Roman and Alex
Cub Scout Pack Pinewood Derby
2018

Roman and Alex
2019

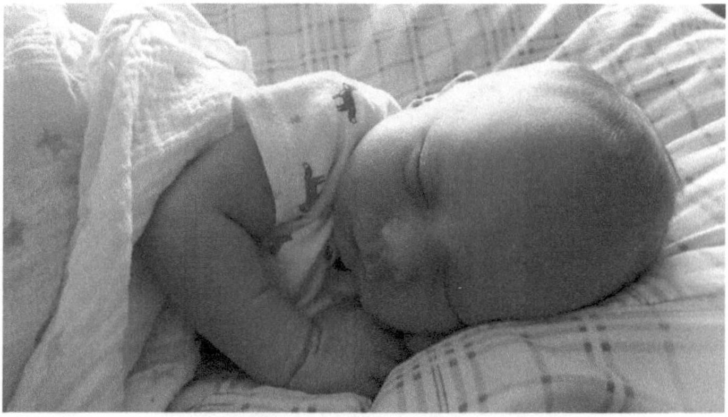

Nathan
2016

Nathan
Christmas
2017

Nathan
2017

Nathan
2018

Ken
Boy Scouts of America
2016

Ken
Lt. Col. Ga. Air National Guard
2002

Chapter 8

The Resurrection of a Scout Troop 1977–1980

Scouting had disappeared in the 1970s from Effingham County, well, at least from Rincon. It's no secret that lack of interest, by Scouts and parents, resulted in many troops closing their doors. I honestly believe the main reason was the Boy Scout Handbook, which had fallen into a city type Scout book. The citified version had left out many things that the old Scout books had taught for many years.

Green Bar Bill Hillcourt rewrote the new Scout handbook that came out about 1989. He introduced a lot of items in the 1989 book that were missing from the citified version. He brought back such things as trail markings, semaphore, Morse code, more leaf and animal identifications, and more outdoor-related information.

But by 1977, Scout Troop 664, sponsored by the Rincon Lions Club, had folded. Its former Scoutmaster had all the equipment stored in his shed. He gave me an old wall tent, an Army medical tarp made out of canvass that weighed a ton, a Boy Scout Troop flag with the numbers 664 on it, and stakes needed to put up the tarp and tent. This was the first troop gear we inherited.

I took the old flag, Troop 664, and cut the "4" out of it on both sides and fabricated a 5 out of white cloth to replace it. I hand sewed the numbers onto the flag, and, well, it looked awful, but that was our flag. The former Scoutmaster also gave me a stand of three pipes that was used to place the flags in when in the field or for a court of honor. It would never stand up. Flags kept falling over, a slight wind, or just any other good reason caused it to tip over. I took the top of one of my bookcases that was round. I chiseled a 5 over the 4 and made a stand that would stand up… if I placed a cinder block on it.

From 1977 to 1993, I had to keep records of all troop activities, attendance, campouts, etc., by pencil. I developed a clever system for tracking merit badges, attendance, advancements, camping trips, and other activities in the record book. I gave each category weighted points and, at the end of each season, usually in July, I tallied up the points for each boy. The top three got medals: Scout of the Year First Place (Gold Medal), Second Place (Silver Medal), and Third Place (Bronze Medal). This was easier to do by pencil than with today's computer systems. Had they asked a Scoutmaster's opinion, they would have added a way to do this in their new computerized system.

Our troop met in an old garage that belonged to the First Baptist Church of Rincon. It faced Richland Avenue. It had a lighted play yard and bleacher seats inside. We had no room for patrol corners, so at each meeting, we'd all meet in one huge patrol corner, collected dues, took roll, and then began training. We started with several basic tasks, such as how to build a fire, how to cook on a grill, and first aid.

Outside, we played games by patrol and many were more physical fitness type tests than Scout skills. We practiced knot tying and had many knot-tying relay races. We met on Tuesday night from 7 – 8:30 PM. This was later changed to Monday night so as not to interfere with high school band practice.

What was noteworthy of Troop 665 was the immediate desegregation within the troop. We had five black Scouts mixed with about twenty-five other Scouts. They were Randy, Clyde, Bernard, Elliott, and Chris, and they were excellent young men of good character. One still seeks me out even today.

Randy J. was a tall boy for his age. Inside the play area of the church was a swing set. This was obviously built for very young and small kids because the seats were less than two feet off the ground. Randy was just sitting in one of the seats, behaving. True, he shouldn't have sat there, but he wasn't roughhousing, he was sitting quietly. All of a sudden, he lost his balance and fell back. He let out a yell and started holding his wrist. Two adults took Randy to his house, picked up his mom, and took them to Effingham Hospital. After X-rays, it was determined Randy had broken his wrist. He only fell two feet and his wrist was broken!

After casting his arm and the gathering of medical information was done, we took Randy and his mom home. That was one of our earliest injuries in the troop. I'll only talk about those injuries of significance as I travel through this chapter.

I must admit that, during the first five years of Scouting, it rained on every camping trip. There was an article in the Effingham Newspaper with the headline "Need Rain? Send Troop 665 on a camping trip!" On our first camping trip to Logs Landing Scout camp, located on Logs Landing Road just outside of Rincon, we set up our campsites in a straight line. This was done in a military style, and was how I thought it should be. In less than a year, Donnie B. came on board and changed all that. Scouts camped by patrols in *Mickey Mouse ears* formation. Each patrol has its own fire and cooking area in a semi-circle, and each patrol can be touching each other or can be scattered several yards apart.

The adults had their own camping area. From those early days on, we always used the two-man rule, so no Scout was left alone with one adult. We practiced youth protection before they called it youth protection. We always had two adults with Scouts, even if they were getting chewed out or had a problem with something in their campsite, like a tent collapsing.

On that first camping trip, we strung up our medical tarp between four trees and planned on teaching first aid under the tarp that night. Rain soon set in and began to wet the tarp and make it stretch. Water began to puddle in the middle, but I ignored it. We were staying dry, so let's train. As we trained, as it rained, we went from sitting to laying on our stomachs to study first aid from our Scout books. I had a lantern under the tarp, in the center. Lower and lower the tarp came down until we were facing out all four directions reading passages on how to treat spider bites, snake bites, sunburn, blisters, scratches, cuts, and other mild first aid problems. It wasn't ideal weather or location for training, but it was all we had at that time. Finally, as we finished up the first aid, one of my Scouts turned to me and said, "Mr. Luikart, you have the patience of a rock." That was quite a compliment, I think.

That night on the camping trip, it was very cold. At night I was looking forward to putting my long-johns on and crawling into my sleeping bag. When I pulled out my long-johns, I had two bottoms. Robert H. laughed himself silly at my predicament. As I was grumbling, he asked me, "Who helped you pack?"

"My wife did," I retorted. He continued to laugh and pulled out his long-johns and he had two shirts. I started laughing then I said, "And Robert, who helped you pack?"

He said, “Brenda.” So we made peace and traded each other one item for the other and finally got to bed and to sleep.

The next morning was cold and clear. The rains pushed through and we were able to get up and start cooking on our grills. We cooked on open fires back then, not the gas stoves we use today. Yes, we still practice cooking on coals or over a fire set on the ground. Stoves are so much easier and less messy. I had finished breakfast when I heard someone from the little Eagles patrol yell out, “Fire!” “Fire!” I glanced over at their cooking area and there was a leaping fire that was about six feet high. It was blazing up from their campfire. I ran over to the patrol with my shovel and took a big hunk of sandy earth and threw it on their skillet. The fire went out immediately, but there in the middle of their fire pit was a skillet with their eggs (all of them) and bacon (all of it) cooking, rather smoldering, in the fire.

I had put the fire out, but now what? In good Scoutmaster fashion, I told them to get a glove and pull the skillet out of the fire. Then to bury its contents, which they did. Then I instructed them to clean their skillet in sand first, to remove gritty burned-on food, and then wash it and rinse in hot water, which they also did. Needless to say, everyone scrounged up enough food to feed the newest little patrol.

That night we played *capture the flag*. In the late 1970s, Logs Landing Road was a dirt road with no traffic. We played on both sides of the road, down by the creek, and into the woods on the southern side of the road. We also played in the road. I split up the patrols and let them choose who was against whom. Of course, the larger boys wanted to outdo the younger boys, so they all stuck together. That meant the little ones were up against bigger boys, some of them six foot tall and 300 pounds.

After losing two games, I decided I'd help the little ones. We came up with a game plan. I'd grab the flag, but they all had to run interference for me so I could escape. "Just get in their way," I told them. The older boys, being smarty pants, put their flag in the middle of Logs Landing Road. They snickered, there was no way anybody was going to get that flag. I had other ideas.

We belly-crawled on our stomachs for about fifty yards, along the creek, into thickets, and across open areas, it was slow going. The other half of the team had hidden their flag behind a large tree and their flag was invisible. Older boys were getting caught trying to find it. We crawled and crawled until I was about thirty feet from the flag. I whispered, "Are you guys ready?" I heard whispers of *yes* and so I sprang into action.

I grabbed their flag before they saw me coming, since it was pitch black. I ran down Logs Landing road, and my thoughts were to turn left, run to the creek and double back, cross the road at a 90-degree angle and touch flags, thus winning the game! I turned left and took off down a path. About five feet down this path, suddenly, there was no earth below me. The Scout chasing me was Ray S., he said he saw me disappear but the flag was left behind. He ran to grab the flag.

I had tumbled into Ebenezer Creek, doing a complete forward somersault, landing on my bottom between numerous cypress knees. Seconds later, a second body crashed down on top of me. We sat there for a minute and then laughed. We had narrowly escaped injury by inches. We had fallen about twenty feet and landed in a deep spot on the edge of the creek. Looking up, I spied the flag, still there, stuck in the branches of the tree above the creek. Needless to say, we quit that game for the night.

We played a lot of games back then, especially spotlight tag. Spotlight tag was less dangerous than capture the flag. In spotlight tag I used a large powerful flashlight and would attempt to find boys evading through the woods. Of course young boys always buy those fancy expensive tennis shoes with reflective designs on them. I'd shine the light down into the woods and see their feet! They were "caught" and came up to help me look for other boys.

On another camping trip, I ran smack into a boy that was about six feet tall and weighed 300 pounds. He was solid as a rock. That hurt, boy did that hurt, he, however, wasn't hurt. On the same night, a Scout ran through our campsites and ran into a rope that was roping off an axe yard. That gave him such a bruise and rope burn it ended the game and another Scouter and myself took him to the emergency room at Effingham. They really grilled us about this injury. The ER people even took a statement from the boy without us being present. I guess they thought we'd hung him with a rope.

On several camping trips that year and the next, we played a game that is now banned. It wasn't mean or hurtful, it was fun and funny to watch. But it's banned. We took the boys on a snipe hunt. Not like you're thinking, no not taking them off into the woods and losing them. No, we gave each new Scout a bag and set them up in the road in a catching position. Ric W., another Assistant Scoutmaster, tied a white hanky onto a black fishing rod and then put the hanky and tip of the road in his pocket. I walked behind him, holding the rod, and had the older Scouts yell "WHOOP! WHOOP! WHOOP!"

As we walked towards the new Scouts, Ric would yell out, "There he goes!" and drop the hanky out of his pocket.

I would start running at the young Scouts while bouncing the hanky and yelling, "Don't let it bite ya, don't let it bite ya."

I'd would run it into a bag and an older boy would pounce on it and say, "I got it, I got it." and Ric would reach in and get the hanky, hide it in his hand and we repeated this several more times.

Finally, tiring of the game, we would all return to camp. We would hide the rod and hanky and when the little ones got to camp, they always found that the snipe had pecked their way to freedom. There were always very disappointed Scouts, there would be no snipe for breakfast. It was harmless fun, but considered as harassment by BSA Headquarters in Dallas, so we quit playing that game.

We used to play British Bull Dog on cold nights when everyone wore their thick jackets and were well padded. This game is banned now by Scouting, but for boys it was a lot of fun. The game started with one or two Scouts in the middle. These guys would try to catch the others as they ran by. They had to pick them up, count, "One, two, three, British Bull Dog," where they were unceremoniously dropped to the ground. Those boys, in turn, would then be part of the catching team. Object of the game? Be the last one caught. Remarkably, no Scout was ever seriously injured playing this game. The winner would usually be an Effingham varsity football player. But alas, we are no longer allowed to play that game, either. However, we still play Steal the Bacon, Capture the Flag, Kick the Can, Bear, and Spotlight Tag.

One day, the Baptist Church said we had to move. They were tearing down the old garage we'd been meeting in to build a new youth building. (It later served as a funeral home for Strickland's for several years after it was built). We had to move, so we moved to the Hinley building. The building was the community center and location of the Rincon Volunteer Fire Department. The building was larger inside, and had seating, but the outside lighting was limited and the building was very close to Georgia Hwy 21.

The first Christmas in this building, I got the bright idea to stuff a piñata with candy, bust it wide open and have the boys scramble for candy. So I found one, a donkey, and I stuffed it with lots of candy. I mean it was *stuffed*. I hung it from the ceiling by a rope and found a broom stick to burst it.

The Senior Patrol Leader blindfolded a Scout and spun him three times. He gave him the stick and sort of guided him to the donkey. He swung wildly at that paper animal, hitting it several times, which caused boys to surge forward. On one of his wild swings, he missed El Pedro and hit Kenny J. in the eye. This blacked Kenny's eye immediately. I stopped the game and broke open the donkey by hand, while other leaders found ice for Kenny.

The second year I tried it again. Trying out a different shape, I think it was an egg or something, I filled it with candy and hung it up in the Hinley building. This time I was going to use a new broom handle and give it to the Senior Patrol Leader and have him bust it with eyes open. I made every Scout back up against the wall, far from the piñata, and asked the Senior Patrol Leader to begin whacking at it. *Whack, whack, whack, whack,* and then the tip broke off the broom handle, flew across the room and hit Kenny in the eye, blacking his eye. Again, I felt so terrible and was so mad that stick broke.

I had a hard time convincing Kenny's mom to let him stay in Scouting. He did stay.

Eventually, we had to change sponsors and change locations – again. Pastor Ricky Varnell invited our troop over to the Rincon United Methodist Church, and we changed sponsors about 1980. We met in the old Methodist Church building, which had a small room at the back, which we used as an office. In there, we kept merit badge books and troop flags and patrol flags. In the old sanctuary area was a large open room. In that room, each patrol could have its own table for a patrol corner. This worked out well. We had an old gas stove that we lit for every meeting during cold weather. Plus, we had a large, well-lit area to play outside. Well, it was sort of big.

Twice my truck window was broken playing dodge ball or football. Twice I replaced my front windshield. Once I was playing touch football and cutting to my left when I ran my hand through one of the church's classroom windows. Outside of those small details, it was perfect.

Again, I was going to do the piñata at the Christmas party, only the right way. I bought a feeble looking piñata, filled it with candy and hung it by a rope in the center of the old Methodist Church building. I took my aluminum ball bat. No more broken sticks, and no more whacking that stupid thing till your arm was tired. No, I was going to bust this thing open with one mighty swing!

I put Kenny in a safe place, slightly behind me and way far away against the wall. All the boys were up against the wall, no one was to move until I popped that thing open. I grabbed my bat and took a stance. I took careful aim and, I had some velocity in those days. I whacked that piñata with a mighty yell and a mighty blow. With one whack, I had split that thing wide open and candy flew everywhere! Boys ran in and a great melee began in the middle of the room. The last thing I saw was little Kenny on the bottom of the pile, looking up when a big boy's knee smashed him in his eye and blacked his eye. From that Christmas onwards, we played bingo. And we refuse to play any other game for fear of injury and black eyes.

While at the old Methodist Church, we used to do first aid drills. I would take an old chicken bone, broke it and taped it onto a Scout's leg. I made blood out of Karo syrup and red food coloring. This had the remarkable consistency of real blood. It also looks like blood. I would take the syrup and pour it generously on the boy's legs, socks, shoes, and pants. I'd have him yell and scream in pain as the Scouts would find him and immediately go to their Scout handbooks to find out what to do for a compound fracture. I did this with arms, ankles, and legs. We had plenty of ripped up sheets and other bandages for use to properly stop bleeding, immobilize the leg, and call 911.

Sometimes, it was first aid for a bloody nose or a knocked-out tooth, teaching them about putting a busted out tooth into a glass of milk and taking it to the dentist to be put back in place. We had first aid training for a stick in the eye, and what to do for automobile accidents with multiple victims. We talked about broken bones and blood, and different problems to make them think. Sometimes we laid a rope across a car accident to teach them to look and assess the scene before you go flying in. The rope represented a live wire, which could electrocute them.

Inside the old church, we had something called Three Seconds to Think training. The Scouts were given scenarios that had to be solved quickly, such as finding and retrieving a stricken Scout from a pretend burning building while blindfolded. What do you do? The blindfold made it very difficult and represented smoke. We taught the fireman's carry, the two-man carry and other ways to carry an injured person.

Well, one day, someone from the church was checking on us. We had locked our backroom because we had money in there, and other things that we didn't want pilfered or left to possible vandals who got into the church. The lock prevented them from going into the room, so they went to the side window and found something to stand on to look into our office window. They spied a large bowl in the middle of a table with numerous wrappings covered in what they thought was blood and chicken bones, also covered in blood.

I was immediately contacted by the pastor and was asked about the blood and bones in the back room.

Someone in the church wanted to know if we were practicing some type of voodoo! I explained to him what we did with the blood and bones, and thankfully, that was the end of that. Those responsible will remain unnamed.

We have had a long existence with the church, probably close to forty years. In those years, they have fully supported us and we have maintained our Scouting values of Duty to God, Duty to Country, and Duty to Yourself. Those are the aims of Scouting in a nutshell.

About 1979, we visited the Okefenokee Swamp State Park. We saw a snake show, and alligators, and walked the swamp boardwalk. Finally, we were going up into the observation tower, probably an old fire tower that gave you a fantastic view of the swamp. The lady picking up trash and litter stopped us and gave us a briefing on park etiquette, about throwing litter on the ground and trashing up the park. She handed out a one-page synopsis of the swamp, and a map of the area. I was thinking the anti-litter speech was about not throwing those papers on the ground – put them in the trash, where they belong. I looked down and she was picking up trash with her stick. It had a nail on the end to stab garbage with.

So single file, we went up the steps to the tower. Winding back and forth, it was taking some time to reach the top. All of a sudden, I saw a perfectly formed paper airplane come sailing by. Around and around it went, with some uplift it was floating perfectly, around and around and around until it hit the lady picking up the trash in the back of the head with the sharp point. Startled, she looked at the paper airplane, and then looked up the tower. At that point, I knew we were in trouble.

At the top of the tower, I asked who'd made the plane and launched it. Charley P. answered, "I did Mr. Ken, I'm sorry." The damage was done, and I told Charley to apologize, and our troop would suffer the consequences. Charley did, and we ended up doing a one hour trash and grounds clean up at the state park. It was embarrassing, but ten times worse because she was holding a bag of trash in her hands from her morning trash pickup.

In 1979, we wanted to set up a place to swim in the lake near Laura S. Walker State Park. We chose our lifeguard, our spotter on the bank, and adult supervision. The older Scouts and adults walked the lake from shore out to chest high. Of course, we were wearing shoes just in case of broken glass or stumps. We set that up as the outer boundary. No one was to go beyond the weighted milk bottles we put out.

We came back in and made a swimming area from waist high out to the milk bottles. The area between the inner bottles and the shoreline was the beginner's and non-swimmer's area. The water was dark and black looking. You couldn't see the bottom. This was 1979, and no one feared alligators at all, they were scarce. We had a lot of fun that afternoon with our safe defense swim setup. This was one of maybe three times we set up one of these swimming areas. Today I would not do it. It's too risky; we have allowed the gators to take back and control all of our interior lakes and waterways.

Chapter 9

The Growing Up Years 1981 – 1995

Some of our activities began to change as we matured as a Scout troop. I wanted to always challenge the Scouts with something clever. Jamey had a stuffed dog named Henry. As he grew older, I asked him if I could borrow Henry for a game. I took Henry, a yellow dog with floppy ears, to a Scout meeting and held him up at the end of the meeting and stated, "This is Henry. He belongs to Jamey, my son, and Henry gets lost a lot. Your quest for the next couple of weeks is find Henry and bring him to Scouts and present him to me. Everyone nodded and agreed they would find him quick.

I took Henry to the flower shop on Highway 21. It's now an event building but still has the lighted bell loft windows. I asked the owner of the shop if Henry could sit up there and she agreed. She said, "But what if they come in and say, 'Hey, we see Henry in the window.' What do I do then?"

I said, "Just let them climb up and get him down, that's all." Henry sat up there so majestically, I figured they would spot him in a couple of days. The next meeting rolled around and Henry was still missing. I encouraged them to try harder, maybe walk the streets, keep looking. Well, week two came and went and still no Henry. I said to them that Henry was really wanting to come back home, please look for him.

The third week, I got a call from the florist, "They found him! They finally spotted him! Several boys came in and asked to get him down, and I said 'Yes' and they took him down and carefully carried him away." They brought Henry to Scouts and he was reunited with Jamey with great joy.

This gave way to an annual lost child hike. The purpose of this was to train the Scouts to search for a missing person. In 1978 or 79, I built a life-size dummy. I found a pair of coveralls, formed a spongy head and face and filled him with shipping peanuts. I called him Rodney. Over the last four decades, Rodney has hidden in many places, many ravines, tangles, briars, and street corners. But, there was a time before Rodney when I needed a real child for a lost child hike.

My daughter, Jennifer, was born in the summer of 1981. She was born in the old Telfair Women's Hospital, located in Candler Hospital, Savannah. We hadn't had a Luikart girl born into our immediately family since about 1949. At least in our immediate family that was a Luikart. I told the doctor there was no way I was having a daughter, it was a going to be a boy. We even picked out his name and clothes he was to wear home.

The due date was preplanned since this would be Sandi's second C-section. That made life a little more predictable, albeit to Sandi's worry of another surgery. So, on the appointed day in July 1981, we went to the hospital for the arrival of our next son. Jamey was excited to get a brother and my family expected another boy.

After a short while in surgery, where Sandi was awake and could hear everything, the baby was delivered. Sandi was sewn up and a baby girl was laid upon her chest. She was so excited, but we hadn't talked about girl's names, just boy's names. So, Andrew was a female in search of a name. I am not totally sure how we came up with her name, but we decided on Jennifer Brooke Luikart. We thought the name was pretty, and unique. However, I honestly believe there were thousands of Brookes born that year.

She was placed in an incubator and wrapped up in white blankets. The doctor personally rolled Jennifer out to meet me in the hall. I looked down at this tiny little baby with a perfect round head and wondered about his future. The doctor looked at me and said, "Mr. Luikart look here..." he flung the blanket aside and there was a girl underneath! Not a boy. I was dumbfounded. *A girl?* I actually had a baby girl. Then the thought came to me that she was going to grow up spoiled. Well, a little anyway.

Her first year of life was touch and go for us, she was diagnosed as having Sudden Infant Death

Syndrome (SIDS). We finally received a monitor from Lockheed, but the first night alone, Jenny had over seventy instances where she stopped breathing for more than thirty seconds. The alarm was placed above our heads in the bedroom and when she stopped breathing the alarm would scream and wake us up.

We started leaving the light on and playing the radio in her room. We didn't walk around her quietly; we wanted her sleep somewhat disturbed. We even had a monitor for our car, and when we went to Savannah, we had to make sure she was hooked up properly. After her first birthday, the monitor was taken off and she was allowed to sleep normally. As she got older, she started to pull on the wires breaking them. The alarm would go off, and she would get a parent to come and see about her. She knew that pulling on those wires would quickly get attention from an adult. Unfortunately, when she pulled on those small wires it would often cause them to break. Robert H. would solder the wires back together for us, a fist full at a time, saving us a lot of money.

While Jennifer was a baby, we lived on West Johnson Street. My mother and father-in-law built an extra room onto the house and we lived together for several years. It's never a good idea to live with your parents or in-laws, but it saved us money, as I was working the forty hour week and Sandi was working part time. Sandi actually wanted to be a stay-at-home mom and we made ends meet so she could be there for the kids as they grew up.

The house we lived in on West Johnson Street was not known to be haunted, but strange things happened that cannot be explained. One story comes to mind, a true story that I cannot explain to this day. It was a Saturday morning, early in the morning, probably 7:00 a.m., when I heard a cupboard door open in the kitchen. Then it shut. A second door opened and then a few seconds later it shut. I was becoming annoyed. I thought it was Sandi's mom or dad looking for something in the kitchen cupboards. Again, a door opened and shut.

I rolled over to Sandi and I said, "What on earth are they looking for."

Sandi was still sleepy and said, "Who, Ken? What are you talking about?" We both heard another cupboard door open and shut. Sandi whispered to me, "Ken, Mother and Daddy are over in Beaufort visiting Aunt Jane and Uncle Shorty!" I was stunned.

I got up, quickly grabbed my Mosin Nagant rifle, with a flip-out bayonet, and fixed bayonet. I crept down the hall expecting to see a burglar. I peeked into the laundry room. No one was there, nor was there anyone in the kitchen.

We discussed this among the adults but never told the kids. Sandi and I wondered if that house was haunted, or maybe someone that lived there had passed away and was visiting. We don't know, but one thing we do know is those solid wood doors were opening and being forcefully shut. That was not a dream, it was real and it scared us. I have no explanation as to who, or what, was opening and closing those cupboard doors.

You may not think that National Security, and the relationship between Boy Scouts and the US Army would cross paths, but it did. In 1983, the Coastal Empire Council had a very large camporee. They spread Scout troops all over Hunter Army airfield. We were given a site that was down the northern perimeter road, near the ammo bunkers.

We were set up and had our kitchen boxes put up, and the Scouts were getting snacks and settling in for the weekend when there was a runner from the council going from troop to troop informing everyone of an emergency Scoutmaster's meeting.

Curious about what was going on, Donnie and I went to the meeting, and were told, "You have exactly ninety minutes to break your camp, pack up your gear, and vacate Hunter Army Airfield. The Camporee has been postponed."

"Why? What's going on?" came the reply from the haggard Scout leaders.

There was a pause. "Because you are all camped on an ammo dump that is deemed unsafe and could explode at any moment!" was the reply. I was dumbfounded, I'd handled munitions all the time, and… this couldn't be true. What's the deal?

Then came this warning. "If you are not out of here in ninety minutes, we are coming to your campsite with dump trucks and buses, and we will physically remove your tents and gear in dump trucks and put you on buses, and you will be deposited off base." Well, that was a threat. *Ninety minutes?* Man, now we had to hurry back and explain to our Scouts that we had to pack up and leave, actually be gone, in an hour and a half.

Of course, everyone asked me why, and I told them what I knew. "We are camped on the ammo dump and it's unstable. Start packing." To my surprise, the Scouts were out of there and on their way home in forty-five minutes. Later that night, the U.S. Army Rangers camped in our campsites and left the next day to invade Grenada. The rest is history.

In 1985, we bought a house on Middleton Drive. Our first real home that belonged to Sandi and me was bought fourteen years after our marriage. It was a nice home built on a large lot with plenty of kids next door. Some were okay kids, some were a little more testy, but we were glad our two had children to play with.

When we moved into our house the living room and kitchen were done in brown. The living room had brown carpet, the kitchen brown linoleum. The walls were dark brown paneling and the kitchen had dark brown cabinets. We had brown furniture, which after it was all placed into the house looked like we lived in a cave. We lived like this for a little while but it drove us crazy living in such a dark and cave-like area.

Finally, on one deployment, I went overseas and Sandi decided to put up wallpaper that was light colored in the living room and kitchen. Then she had a carpenter add a chair rail, had the carpet replaced, and the kitchen floor linoleum replaced with a lighter tan. When she finished her remodeling, we had enough money to buy new furniture. A nice bright-looking couch and easy chairs. Sandi had created a bright living area all by herself. It became a trademark of my deployments. I was off doing my job for my country, and she was spending money on upgrading the house.

Jamey and Jenny learned to ride bikes on Middleton Drive. Jamey's first time on a bike was perfect. He stayed upright, riding down the road perfectly, and without braking or swerving. Then, he rode right into the back of a car. That was an embarrassment, but he was fine and the car was not damaged. However, later on when new people moved into that house, Sandi somehow ran over their mailbox, destroying the post and the box. Later that evening, I replaced Roger L.'s mail box and post and apologized. It was how we first met. Later on Roger and I would be partners in running Troop 665.

One morning Jenny woke up and, at breakfast, started telling us about the nightmare she'd had the night before. I guess she saw a piece of a King Kong movie, or something on a cartoon show, which showed a large gorilla chasing people. She wanted to tell the whole story from the beginning to end, so we sat back and let her talk. She told us she was exploring around the house or yard, or somewhere, when a large gorilla started chasing her. It was a lively story of near misses and the gorilla almost catching her until she was trapped and had no escape.

"Go on Jenny, how did you escape?"

Swallowing her cornflakes, she calmly said, "I don't know, Daddy, we broke for a commercial."

I blinked, and we burst out laughing. My child has commercials in her nightmares.

Jenny and a friend used to put on plays in her room or on the back porch. If Jenny was alone, she would put on a one person play. She played all of the parts, the dastardly mean man, the helpless lady, and the cowboy that would ride in to save her. Using hats and her finger for a mustache, she created a story about a young woman who couldn't pay her bills. The dastardly mean man forced her out of her off her farm and tied her up on the rails of the local railroad. He demanded payment for her life. The hero, hearing of this, rode in and fought off the mean man and saved the girl just in time. Well, I thought, she's a chip off the old block for sure.

When Jennifer was six or seven and Jamey was in Scouts, I asked Sandi if Jennifer could be the lost child for the lost child hike. I had just written an emergency operations checklist for a lost child. The Scout Troop had never hunted a real person before this exercise. Sandi agreed and dressed her in warm clothes and placed her on cardboard that would help keep her warm.

Sandi sat in the car and observed her. The car was available if Jenny got cold or bored with the game.

At Scouts, I told them a little girl was missing and was dressed in pink. She had a lavender bicycle. They only had the ninety minutes to find her, and she could be anywhere on the west side of Rincon. After a briefing, the patrols broke up and began the entire search of all of Rincon.

About forty-five minutes into the search, the younger Scouts were getting restless with the game. Where was this little girl? Was there really a person or was it a trick to get them to walk all over Rincon and expend energy? Finally, one Scout had to go to the bathroom. There were no stores open so he could pee, so he ran behind Harden's pharmacy, behind a dempsy dumpster. He was about to unzip his pants when he looked behind the dumpster and there was a little girl lying motionless. He cried out for help and the boys went wild. They had found the lost girl, now they had to perform any needed first aid and treat her for shock.

I was pretty pleased that they found Jennifer because it was a very large and troublesome area to search. After first aid and treating for shock, the game ended back at the old Methodist church. We had a critique of the game and search methods and from that game I wrote a little mobilization paper on how to organize the troop for searching for a real lost child in Rincon. We have never had to use it for real, thank goodness, but we practice it once a year with our dummy, Rodney.

Jennifer grew up tall and strong. She picked up an ability to perform in front of an audience without being shy. She was quite the performer. We soon realized she was capable of singing in tune with recordings at a very young age. Sandi wanted her to take dance lessons, so she signed up for local dance classes which she took throughout her school years.

Sandi entered her into the 1984 Mini Miss Rincon beauty contest, and Jennifer won. From that day forward, she won many beauty and modeling competitions. She brought home trophies from Savannah, Brunswick, Waycross, and Beaufort, South Carolina, to name just a few. She also won many photogenic and talent contests, and in 1994, she won Miss Effingham Fair Queen. That honor allowed her to ride in the fair parade sitting on the back of a Mazda Miata sports car, after which she cut the ribbon to open the county fair that year.

Her dancing ability, along with her flute playing, acting ability, and her great voice, all led us to believe that she would somehow pursue a career in music. She used her talents as stepping stones to apply for entry into Georgia Southern University. She decided on music education rather than vocal performance as her major. While there, she sang with the Georgia Southern Chorale and acted and sang in several university productions and operas, as well as having the opportunity to sing at the Vatican. I remember watching her perform in The Pirates of Penzance and remarking to Sandi what a voice range she had as a singer.

That voice range, from the low notes of an alto to the high notes of a soprano is the secret to her wonderful, beautiful sound and tone. I am not a music expert. I played trombone in the high school band and I can read the bass clef notes, but I know what I like. Hearing her sing a technically difficult song, from high to low range and with various tempos is a pleasure to listen to.

In 2003, she graduated with a teaching degree in music. She has taught at various grade schools, and middle schools in Effingham County. I think many people are surprised when they hear Jennifer's chorus perform. They are only middle school kids, but they have a very professional sound to their performances.

Standing at almost six feet tall, she commands a certain discipline in her class. The kids do well for her because they love and respect her. She's not a tyrant with grades, but she does demand a minimum of participation. Music isn't a *gimme class*, if you take her chorus class, you're gonna work.

I love Jennifer so much. I know we spoiled her. Well, to a certain degree, after all, she was the first Luikart girl in our family for a very long time. She has Sandi's looks but my temperament. I love her dearly.

After using Jennifer in a lost child hike, and building our dummy Rodney for subsequent hikes, we decided to expand our search area. Later, about 1986, I used the Union Camp Slash Seed Orchard, just behind Rincon off of Carolina Avenue, as a command post for a game hunting for Rodney. Back then, you could drive down

Carolina Avenue, and where it makes a sharp turn, near the Rincon water wells and firehouse, you could cross over the railroad tracks. The road leading to the seed orchard was called "New Road" and cut all the way through the orchards to McCall road.

I set up a small table, issued walkie-talkies, and laid out a stretcher and first aid supplies. I put Rodney in the woods, about 120 feet from the edge of the road. He wasn't hidden, but laying flat on the ground. He's not that hard to see with a flashlight because he is made of blue coveralls. Blue is a color you do not see a lot of in the woods and is easy to spot. I opened my easy chair, along with several other parents, and we watched the Senior Patrol Leader establish a search party.

We were on a tight schedule, they had about ninety minutes to find Rodney, or I would have to call the game. An hour into the game, I was getting upset. My wife drove out to see how things were going and several Scouts got out of her car. Some of the boys were coming back to operations and I could see them lingering along the dirt road. I approached them and asked, "What's going on?"

"Mr. Ken, we can't find him. We have looked and looked and looked and he's not in those woods!"

"You're just not looking good enough. Come on I'll show you where he is."

I stomped down the dirt road, cut into the woods where Rodney lay, lonely and motionless. I counted off my paces, one chain, two chains; okay, he's got to be here somewhere close to this spot. I yelled out, "He's in this area, right where I am standing, spread out and look for him." The Scouts spread out and began to search. Rodney was nowhere to be found. He was not in those woods. I was getting mad now. "Okay, let's head back to camp, it's almost time to go home." I stomped out of the woods, mumbling to myself, embarrassed, and mad. I approached camp and saw someone sitting in my chair. It was Rodney.

I was mad, yet it was funny too. Debriefing the Scouts, I learned two older Scouts had found Rodney and heard my wife coming up the dirt road. They flagged her down and three Scouts got into the back seat. One of them was Rodney, she never knew and brought the boys back to camp. I don't think she realized she had Rodney until they placed him in my seat. Well, I was fooled and that was a win for the Scouts.

In the mid-80s we found a tract of Union Camp land adjacent to Old Augusta Road, not far from the intersection of Old Augusta and Cherry Hill roads. This was known as the "Sheffield" tract, Ogeechee Forest. The land was about 1,000 acres and ran along the east side of the road. We had a small dirt road that turned off of Augusta road.

Loblolly trees were machine planted some eighteen years earlier and were averaging seven to twelve inches in diameter and about forty-five to sixty feet tall. It was excellent tree-growing soil, a moderately well to well-drained soil on top of red clay. We laid off our campsites in small circular patterns and partitioned them with hanging small trimmed trees from pine to pine, making a one pole fence around the campsite. The boys laid off main trails with logs and we had trails coming from the main trail to each campsite.

Within each camping area, we had room for about five tents, with the fire placed in the center, and the kitchen box near the center as well. There was room for a canopy, or dining fly, in the center of the camp. Each patrol set up their own tents, established their own kitchen area and dining fly. Each patrol was responsible for cleaning up a spot for their fire and axe yard. Axe yards were usually four trees spaced far enough apart to store fire wood, axes, and hatchets.

I liked this setup, it allowed us to go camping at a safe spot, among the woods, with no interference. The first time we visited this site was probably around 1981. Donnie B. and I had gone in the woods earlier and established each patrol's campsite by using a compass to lay off a "5" leg angle and paceline to the campsite. This meant you shot an azimuth with the compass, paced the distance (usually 200-300 feet) to a spot, shot a second azimuth and paced, and so on until you arrived at your camping spot. Here would be a small pink ribbon with the patrol name written on it. Hopefully, it was your patrol.

The Scouts took control of this piece of land. They made steady improvements on this tract of land for several years, until it was harvested. We explored every inch of our tract of land and found, near a wet bottom, an old still. It had axe marks in the sides of the old kettle, and the tubing was smashed, and the entire spot was wrecked. All of us decided it was an old still, and historical, we left it in place. I doubt it's still there.

Near the campsites, north of the area was a borrow pit. This is a large dugout area used to build up a road, to build up a bridge, or to shore up a very muddy, sandy, wet road. The pit was probably fifteen feet deep, with the west end cut away so trucks could come and go. The semi-circle pit was perfect for plays, campfires, and Junior Leadership Training classes. At night we built a large campfire in the center of the pit, Scouts would sit on the bank or bring a chair, and we did skits for hours. On Sunday mornings, we held church there. I would dig through the Bible and find scriptures from the Old Testament that pertained to the weekend. We had Jewish, Methodist, Baptist, Church of God, Mormon, and Presbyterian Scouts and adult leaders. In honor of all the religions, I kept devotions to books like Job, or Proverbs. Sometimes Psalms, especially some of the things that David wrote about our relationship to God. In a way, this was a very special place in my heart. I miss it today.

The next year, 1987, we went to Camp Daniel Boone for our summer camp. The lake water was super cold, but we got to white water raft down the Nantahala River on Friday.

The Rincon Church of God let us use their church bus for this trip. One of their church members, who had a boy in our troop, was our driver. The excitement was building as we were heading to the historic Camp Daniel Boone, located in the mountains near Ashville, North Carolina.

The bus chugged out of Rincon; everyone was getting ready for the very long six to eight hour trip. We stopped at Colombia, South Carolina and had a meal, then back on the bus and back on the road. It took forever to get to Daniel Boone and all of us were dead tired when our bus pulled in and stopped. After getting set up, there was enough daylight for our swim test. I went with the boys and when I jumped in the water, it took my breath away. It sucked all the air out of my lungs and I was struggling to breathe. I immediately got out, along with most all the troop. The water was cold, some say it's around forty-seven degrees – even on a sunny day. I couldn't fault the Scouts for getting out if I couldn't take it. Not very many waterfront badges were earned that summer.

During our rafting trip, the school bus was able to follow us down the river, taking pictures of the troop as we hit the last chute on the Nantahala River. This dropped us about ten to fifteen feet and was a hoot. It's fun if you don't capsize and get thrown out, and if you do, well then, it isn't a lot of fun at all.

The week went well. We rock climbed and rappelled down a steep cliff. The Scouts earned a lot of merit badges and enjoyed the camp. Tired and wore out, we packed the bus for the trip home Saturday. We expected a long trip, so we tried to leave early to arrive in Rincon, about 4:00 o'clock pm.

The bus began to shudder and clank, and it was roaring. To me, it sounded like a manifold problem, but homeward bound we went. Somewhere near Tyrone, North Carolina, the bus engine seized up, and we stopped on the roadside. The poor old church bus had died and now we were on I-26 stranded on the interstate. Not long after, we all disembarked and sat across the ditch, a North Carolina Highway Patrol came by and stopped.

He got a local church to come pick us up and take us to the next exit, where we could eat and rest. The bus was towed to a garage not far from the exit. We waited and waited and waited. We waited so long that one Scout said "I'm walking home, I don't care about what anybody says!" And just like that, he was heading up a bank into some planted pines and had disappeared. I turned to the Senior Patrol Leader and said, "Take four boys and bring him back, either on his own or carry him back and sit on him, we're not losing anyone."

Off they scampered up the bank and into the woods. We all turned our heads and backs away from the woods so we didn't hear what happened. Several minutes later, the boy was coming back on his own and sat down. I didn't say anything, but watched as the older boys got him a drink and sat down near him to make him feel better. It was a tough time just waiting, we waited probably three hours when a young Methodist minister drove up in an air-conditioned church bus. He said to me, "Let's load up and have them get snacks to eat on the bus and we will press on for Rincon.'

"Get snacks? On your bus?"

"Yes," he said.

The boys loaded up on french fries, pie, and drinks, and we loaded our gear on his bus. As we sat down in our seats, he turned on the AC, and we even had a video movie. Each seat had a TV mounted above it. To be honest, I couldn't believe how fortunate we were to have a church that was willing to take us home to Rincon. I offered to buy the minister a motel room, but he said no, it was okay, he was driving back that same night. He wouldn't even take money to pay for his gas.

We arrived, most were asleep, comfortable, and in good shape, considering our day. I thanked the young bus driver many times, that was the best bus trip I had ever taken, and his kindness was truly that of a Christian.

Meanwhile, back up in Tyrone, North Carolina, the old church bus never started, or moved one foot, ever again. The bus driver called the Church of God in Rincon and asked to junk the bus. I think it was junked up there and our driver was able to get a ride home later. I felt bad about their bus, but it just could not take the mountains.

The next year, in November 1987, Sandi and I and the kids made the yearly trek back home to Nitro, West

Virginia. That same year my sister in law, Wendy, and Dana, made the journey from Virginia to West Virginia. We all met up at Terry and Dave, my sister-in-law and brother's house, up Morgan's Creek. It was rare for all of us to be free from work and holiday worries and gave us a free Saturday to go on a hike. This hike would be labeled the Samuel Rust hike and the mission was to find and investigate the Sam Rust property and cemetery.

Early on a bright, sunny, cool Saturday morning, we gathered at the old house up Morgan's Creek and planned our hike. Sandi and Terry opted out, they didn't want to tackle the hills and we all had kids that needed watching. We did add Jamey and Stan, David's son, to the hike because they were Boy Scouts and they wanted to hike the ridgelines with us.

I found a large 2-liter empty bottle that we tied a rope to and I carried that as a backpack full of water. We had several day packs with snacks, first aid kit, compass, camera, knife, and other odds and ends we used along the trail. One of the highlights of this hike was my brand new RCA video camera. With the shoulder strap tethered in place, I let Dana or Dave trade off carrying it, but I shot a lot of the footage on the videotape. This tape, labeled the "Samuel Rust Hike" is a classic.

We all fell in double or single file and headed down Cardinal Road to the intersection of Morgan's Road and Cardinal Road. Along the way, the creek was rambling pretty good, making its falling water sound as we headed west. The hills were bursting with the late fall colors, almost gone, of yellow, scarlet, red, and many variations of shades of yellow and red pigment left behind in the leaves. It was a beautiful panorama of color and shapes of trees which added a nostalgic feel to the hike.

Reaching Morgan's Road, we turned left and marched about twenty yards to a large standing green rock. The face of the rock facing the road was smoothed and had an inscription in it, "S R" for Samuel Rust. He lived in the cornfield area over near Lock Seven, along the Kanawha River. That was just over the mountain to our southeast. We discussed this old rock and the Rust family and took some pictures.

David turned us toward Nitro and up the hill we went, passed the old gas house on the left, and an old spring on the right. Around the bend and along the straight stretch, David suddenly headed over the hill to our left. We all followed and I wondered what he remembered that I didn't know. It was a second SR stone, lying in the bottom land where it was placed 150-plus years ago.

We followed the bottom land to a trail that led around the edge of Rydenhour Lake and over to a parking lot. While heading in that direction, David showed us a third stone. All these stones were laid out back when Sam Rust was a farmer. Across the parking lot and up the hill following the power line, we tramped.

Up the hill we went following the power line. I was in my late thirties and Dave was just a tad younger. We suffered proper cardiac-pulmonary training. Essentially, we gasped for air. Struggling uphill, going in a serpentine hike movement, we finally reached the top of the hill, or ridgeline, and collapsed. We probably rested twenty minutes, or so, and began our hike. Looking towards the top of the next hilltop we moaned and groaned our way upward. Finally we reached the top of a second hill. It was probably twenty or thirty feet higher in elevation.

Walking towards the Kanawha River on top of the hill, we found some rocks we could stand on and see everything in East Nitro and across the river. We were able to locate the mouth of the Coal River, where Mary Ingle lost her donkey and warm blankets trying to cross the Coal River. This was back in the 1700s, when few white men lived on this side of the Gauley Mountains. There is a great book titled *Follow the River* by James Alexander Thom, that tells the story of Mary. She was captured by Shawnee Indians on the eastern side of the Blue Mountains of Virginia, taken west along the New, Kanawha, and Ohio rivers to the Scioto River, then north to Chillicothe, Ohio. This was the major home of the Shawnee Indians. There was little love between the Shawnee Indians and English settlers.

I won't go into the book here, for there is a book about this brave woman that you should check out. We discussed some items written by William D. Wintz in his book *Nitro the World War I Boom Town.* Mr. Wintz's book helped solidify some things that David and I had heard about, or at least saw in the woods with our own eyes. That is a second book that everyone needs to purchase for their library.

From this point, we followed the trail slightly uphill to a small cemetery bordered by sandstone markers. Each bearing an SRC on them. Inside the cemetery we found many interesting graves, including Sam Rust's grave. His headstone had been pushed over by vandals. It needs to be put back in place. Two other graves of interest were those of Sam Rust's son James and his best friend, and brother-in-law, Henry Gregory.

James was hiking along the same ridge we were walking. He remarked to a relative that if he should die during the Civil War, he wanted to be buried up on this ridge line overlooking the Kanawha and the mouth of the Coal rivers. James had a friend named Henry Gregory. Henry married James' sister Elizabeth Rust. Ironically both James and Henry joined the confederate army in the 22nd Virginia Infantry Regiment. Both men were killed in August of 1863 and are buried side by side on top of that hill. *(Nitro the World War I Boom Town, William D. Wintz)*

Leaving here we hiked on around the hillside and came down beside the old Shope farm ruins and down by the Moore's house on Morgan Road. Thus, ending a pretty long and tough hike.

In June and July of 1989 Donnie B., Jimmy R., Pete M., and I hosted the 1989 Scout Jamboree. We were all excited about the trip. Ed F. and our committee set up a tremendous trip up the coastal United States to Virginia. We visited several museums and Civil War battlefields. We also planned on visiting the Navy training submarine and maritime museum. We visited Yorktown, Williamsburg, and Mount Vernon, the home of George Washington.

We had constructed a special gateway, for our campsite at the jamboree, of cypress poles. It even included a brilliant rotating light on top that looked like a lighthouse. We all had our soft tote bags, and tents, and kitchen boxes all loaded underneath the bus. We got up and had breakfast at the 165th Services dining hall, had our final safety briefing, and loaded onto the bus. One bus load of forty Scouts, four adult leaders, and one bus driver.

Across the Savannah River, about mile marker 15 in South Carolina, the engine on the bus seized up and we stopped immediately. Our bus was dead in the water. Our driver got help calling for another bus and we unloaded all our gear and lay it in the grass along the interstate. That was an awful feeling. Standing around on the side of the road with all our gear strung out everywhere, some people began feeling a little ill.

I had picked up a box of aircraft air sickness bags. I think there were over 300 bags in that bundle. I hung on to them and the vomit medic for the trip. Luckily while stopped we had use of the bathroom in the rear of the bus. Some boys were already exhibiting diarrhea and an upset stomach. Donnie had been sick the week before, but he was feeling okay and was beyond spreading sickness. Little did I know this was a harbinger of things to come.

The bus showed up and it took us about a half hour to gather up all our gear and load it onto a new bus. Finally, we were ready to go, and with a cheerful face we loaded up and off we went towards Virginia. We suffered through South Carolina into North Carolina. I was passing out sickness bags and they were being filled up quite quickly. The toilet was also being heavily used. Of forty boys on the bus I estimated half of them were hit with vomit and diarrhea. They were lined up to use the bus toilet.

As we went into North Carolina, it was obvious that we had a bug attack among us. What ever virus hit us hit the stomach. Food would not stay down and the Scouts drank a lot of water, but it wouldn't stay down either. Of the 300 vomit bags I had run through half of them.

We stopped for lunch; it was a quick McDonald's meal. It's easier to feed everyone if everyone eats the same thing. Costs go way down and it's much quicker. However, that probably wasn't a good idea as the vomiting and sick stomach followed us into Virginia. The bus toilet was so full of diarrhea and vomit that the bus driver put us all out at a shopping center to go dump the bus toilet. After he cleaned the toilet and added chemicals we loaded and went up the road into Virginia. We stopped at the Coast Guard Academy and unloaded for the night. Scouts were sick and were still vomiting, but we couldn't leave anyone behind.

That evening after supper, we went to Bush Gardens Theme Park to enjoy the rides and eat. A new set of boys became sick and I was almost out of vomit bags. I had about thirty boys sick and a whole batch of boys who had not been sick that morning, but became deathly ill that night. Jamey, my son, missed out on rides because he was vomiting. Inside the theme park, he had to vomit. I told him to go into the bushes behind a bench and stay low, on all fours, and let it all come up. He did, unfortunately a young couple started to use the bench for kissing and cuddling. All of a sudden all you heard from the bushes behind the bench was this huge call for a well-known car. BUICK! BUICK! BUICK!

They were surprised and stood up and walked briskly away. My son stayed in those bushes until a medic arrived and we put about six boys into the parks medical center. The next day, we visited Yorktown and Williamsburg. We still had sickness with us. Then we traveled from Williamsburg to the Washington Zoo, then on to Andrews AFB, Washington. Arriving at Andrews, I had a particular boy that had become extremely sick. He was trying to use the bus bathroom, but had messed his pants. We had enough clothes handy that we got him cleaned up.

When we arrived at the base, they had set up cots for us in the hanger. My sick Scout, the boy that was extremely ill, was trying to hurry to the bathroom. He took a step and vomited, took another step and diarrhea hit the floor. He would take a step and vomit then take a step and mess the floor. We followed him into the bathroom and put him, clothes and all, into the shower. Meanwhile, the other ten or so Scouts became very ill and started vomiting in the men's restroom filling every sink and toilet with vomit. They tried to clean it up but it was an awful mess. The shower was in the female restroom, so we left our Scout in the shower and went to clean up the mess in the men's room.

About ten minutes later, just as we cleaned up the last sink the boys came running in, "Mr. Ken they are in the girl's bathroom throwing up!" We rushed across the hall into the female restroom and there was every sink, every toilet, and our Scout in the shower stall to clean up. Needless to say, I called the boy's dad, who was a doctor, and told him I had given him Tylenol, and clear liquids, I think it was ginger ale. His dad was *okay, that's good, what did I think about waiting till the next day before bringing him home?* I said *yes that was a good plan*. But if he got worse, we were prepared to take him to the hospital.

Well, the boy got better. And by the time we had finished walking DC and visiting Mount Vernon, everyone was on the mend. When we finally got to the Jamboree site, we stopped and checked in with medical. When we gave them our horrifying story, they quarantined us. That next morning, they gave everyone cereal and milk for breakfast. No one ate. There was no way we were drinking milk, so we sat all of it out by the flagpole to be thrown away. Unfortunately, the Virginia health inspector came into our campsite and when he spied the milk, he climbed all over us. Claiming our boys were sick because of sour milk. We tried to argue, but by this time we, the adults, were getting sick.

Finally, one old Scoutmaster came to see me and said I should require every boy to go wash his clothes and himself in the showers with soap. Rinse out the clothes, and hang them up to dry, and put them all to bed. I did that, meanwhile, our fire buckets became puke buckets and every tent had a puke bucket assigned to it. We also had a designated puke dump-site out behind our camp and we constantly went around and picked up and dumped vomit behind our campsite in the brush.

With lots of soapy water, we showered, washed clothes, and broke the virus. By Tuesday afternoon and Wednesday morning, we were all healed and ready to go. By the way, I had zero vomit bags left and all puke buckets remained at the ready for the rest of the week. But we didn't need them. The trip home was uneventful.

In the early 90s, about December 1992, I was at Air Command and Staff College. This was necessary for me to attend in order to advance to the rank of Lieutenant Colonel. I only had my two-year degree in Forest Technician, and I couldn't work on my Bachelor of Science degree until I finished this military school. The school was located at Maxwell Air Force Base in

Alabama. Unfortunately I had to attend in residence, so we went to Montgomery and found a small apartment, with a Murphy Bed, and a large closet area, at an affordable cost.

My first day of class was the Introductory day. Each student stood up, gave his name and a history of his academic accomplishments, and military history. I was listening intently and it was the same story for each cadet. "My background is a BS in Electronics and a Masters in Mathematics" Oh, I knew I was in trouble. I was a flunk-out at West Virginia State, a Vietnam veteran, an enlisted man for eleven years, and a Forest Ranger. I was a dirt poor candidate, probably the least desirable for this class.

Soon it was my turn and I had to think quick. "I was born a twin. My daddy took both of us fishing one day, but my twin brother caught the mumps. They fell on him while he was in the boat and it rocked the boat and he fell in and drowned. Before my daddy could get back to shore, my momma ran off with the next-door neighbor. Daddy got mad, ran into the house, stuck the shotgun out the window and killed the best breedin' bull in the county. This upset the cow so bad she quit given milk. Daddy lost the farm and all his money and ended up with nothing but his Waterbury watch, an outhouse, and a box of ex-lax. He spent the rest of his life winding his watch and runnin' to the outhouse." I sat down.

The class was stunned. A female major next to me said, "Oh my God, that's terrible!" Whereupon, an officer from Mississippi looked at me and busted out laughing. Even though he was black, we had so much in common. He became a good friend. I never again had to give my spiel on all the accomplishments I achieved in life. It was a given, I would be trouble.

At this same time, about December 1992, Donnie was the acting Scoutmaster for a year until I completed Air Command and Staff College in June 1993. Donnie had his hands full with Scouts that always tested the boundaries of discipline. Donnie was good at keeping the Scouts under control, but it seemed like things happened that scared the dickens out of him.

In January 1993, at the annual Father-Son Freeze Out (Now called the Parent-Pal Freeze Out), the troop set up their tents for a quiet fun weekend. On the way into Blue Heron, an ice storm hit. It's like snow, but its rain freezing on limbs and the road, and bushes and grass and it makes a slippery, glittery, mess.

I'm sure it was getting dark when they set up their tents and built a fire. Everyone was getting settled when a large "crack" was heard, and a huge oak limb, several hundred pounds in weight, crashed down on one of the Scout's tent. It smashed his tent, and all his belongings completely flat. That episode caused Donnie to turn gray, and he prayed that was the end of that kind of problem, however, after resetting the tent up, no one felt safe going to bed.

The next morning, the daily events went off pretty much as expected. Scouts and their parents could compete in a variety of games such as Nose Knows, a game where you use your nose to recognize liquids or solids in each container. Know your Knots was a game our Scouts could usually win, and a host of other games such as match splitting, compass course, ring toss, and so on. After a long day, everyone was told to meet back at camp around 5:00 o'clock for supper. Supper went well; I'm sure they were getting ready for dressing up in uniform for the campfire later that night.

Around one campfire sat a Scout who was wondering what an empty bug spray can would do in a fire. I'm almost positive he was hiding the fact that he had been spraying bug spray into the fire like it was a flame thrower. Now, I knew this boy; he was not evil, just a typical boy that was getting away with stuff we hoped to catch. With the can empty, he decided to toss it into the campfire.

Donnie and the other adults were resting up and getting ready to go to the big campfire. That's when it happened. KA-BOOOOM! A huge explosion rocked the camp. It was a frightening explosion that scared many of the boys that were not paying attention to the bug can being tossed in the fire. When Donnie arrived, there was no campfire, there were no logs in the campfire, and there was only bare ground smoking from the heat. The entire campfire was blown out of the fire pit and scattered in a circle, hundreds of feet away. The fire was out, all of it, blown out by the explosion. The boys around the campfire were blown backwards, in a reclining position, and were stunned by the noise and shock wave.

Donnie lit into them. "Who did this? What did you do? Tell me now, what did you do?" One Scout sheepishly admitted he was responsible, that he had thrown an empty mosquito spray can into the fire. I'm afraid the adults read him the riot act. They yelled at him all weekend, and were so upset, yet thankful no one had been injured. Unfortunately that Scout quit Scouting. He never came back.

After I returned from school, Donnie retired from Scouting as an Assistant Scoutmaster and continued on as an Eagle Scout adviser. I picked up Roger L. in the early 1990s, about 1993 I think, and he was with me for almost fifteen years as my helper.

In the early 90s, we had several Scouts who continued their jealous differences for a while. Two of them were the same age and had come over from the pack at the same time. During summer camp setup, at Camp Blue Heron, campsite #8, two Scouts got into a shoving match. One shoved one way, the other shoved back. They knocked over bunks and the tussle was turning into a fistfight. We broke it up and calmed them down. Then I explained that, when you sin, or do something bad, there are consequences. I told them that I loved them both but I had to make sure they did not fight anymore that week.

I ordered up about 8' of 1/2" rope. I tied one end to one Scout, and the other end to the other Scout. "Here, you will have to wear this while in camp, except in the dining hall and in the latrines. Outside of that, you better be wearing this rope or I'll ding you for poor Scout spirit. After about an hour, I took it off of them and I had no more trouble out of them, or any other Scouts that weekend.

Chapter 10

The Tough Years 1996–2005

In 1994, we made a tough decision based on our summer camping experience at Blue Heron. That was the year the council used the Youth Detention Camp boys as merit badge counselors. I could not stay the weekend, but Roger and Bill F. were in camp and they had their hands full. That was the year that Roger took a different boy, every day, to the local hospital for shots for lockjaw. He was fit to be tied.

During the day, the Scouts were complaining that several of the YDC counselors had gotten into a fight. One hit the other in the head with a flashlight and split his head open. My Scouts were not happy. Also, it seemed the young adult leadership was very grouchy and they were picking on the Scouts. I know this for a fact as one came into our campsite (who shall not be named) and was ragging on the Scouts in our campsite. I stopped dead in my tracks and Roger yelled at him to get out of our campsite and don't come back.

It was getting toward supper and time to dress for lowering the flag. I asked Roger how it went. He muttered and was not happy at all. Bill verified that there were fights, and that the camp seemed unorganized and "hateful." We did not raise a big stink over this, but quietly discussed our next move. Next year we were going somewhere else to summer camp. We would not subject our Scouts to that type of situation again. At least being out of council we might garner a little more respect.

The next year, 1995, we went to Camp Bob Harden, located near Saluda, North Carolina. We rafted the Nantahala River and tubed the Green River. The Scouts enjoyed the mountains and the way the camp was designed around the lake. However, the dining hall was on top of the hill. We called the road up to the dining hall *cardiac hill*. We had to climb that road at least three or more times a day. It was while walking this road when a Scout walked into a slimy mud hole and stopped, looked at me, and asked, "Is this what they call mud?"

In November of 1996, we were invited to Shane A.'s property to camp and do pioneering. The leaves were changing, the air crisp and cool, the sky sunny. We had a great time camping and cooking. We built two tall signaling towers. After they were completed, I had one tower send the second tower a signaling flag message. It took the Scouts a while to figure out the correct flag positions, but using the white and red flags, they transferred the message.

The receiving team decoded the flag messages and learned the importance of understanding flag signals that can be sent from one hilltop to another. We also practiced wigwag flag signals and that night some Morse code. The Scouts loved that camping trip.

So, in November 1997, we scheduled a second pioneering weekend on Shane's property. This was our second camping trip visiting this wooded lot in the middle of Port Wentworth, Georgia. The land was off of highway 80, not far from US 80 and Dean Forest Road. The acreage was plenty big, and was wooded with lots of oak and sweet-gum trees. All we wanted to cut down was available to us.

We set up tents and kitchen boxes, tarps, and prepared for rain. A large rainstorm was moving in on us. We had two young adults with us who watched the troop while Roger, Ric W, and I went to Ric's birthday party at the Mason's Lodge in Savannah. While we were preparing to leave, I told the boys that Shane and Danny W., both over 21, were in camp and that we would return in about two hours. Also, prepare for rain, make sure your sleeping bags are protected from the rain. As we climbed in our vehicles, it started.

It was pouring when we got to Savannah; I was hoping the boys were okay, so I was in a hurry to get back. It poured a frog choker, probably several inches in an hour. What we didn't realize was that this piece of property was lower than all the highways and land around it. Much lower, so low that all the water off the highways poured down into the wooded area and began to flood the campsite.

When we arrived, the boys were sitting on the bank with some of their gear. They were very upset because the storm caught them totally off guard. I looked at Danny, "How bad is it Danny?"

"Oh, Mr. Luikart, it's like Vietnam down there."

I thought for a second, "How deep is it in the campsite?"

"Mr. Ken, the water is up three feet where the fire pit was, your tent is under three feet of water."

I was dumbfounded.

I walked down into the campsite and the water came up to my knees. I went to the tent and my sleeping bag was underwater, soaked. My personal gear was flooded, my axe was underwater, and the entire camp, every tent, was filled with three feet of water.

We had several lanterns lit and I started to return to the Scouts to mitigate the damage. Danny picked up a floating stick and stood in front of a lantern. "Hey Mr. Ken, what's this remind you of?" The lantern cast his dark shadow creeping in knee-deep water and, behind him, the water was giving off something like steam or some kind of water to air exchange.

"Vietnam, Danny, Vietnam! And all this is about as bad as Vietnam."

We called parents to come get us and we called for pick up trucks. We pulled up tents, sleeping bags, tools, patrol boxes, lanterns and everything we could find in the flood and dumped all that gear in the back of trucks. Nothing was packed, it was a mess, a big mess.

The plan was to return to Rincon and unload the gear under the carport at the Methodist Church and spread it out. Everyone was to go home and meet back up on Saturday morning about 9:00 o'clock.

The next morning we began to unravel the mess and claim the tents, sleeping bags, and equipment. Everyone had sleeping bags to clean and tents to wash out and dry. It was a royal mess that stopped us from camping there. We never went back to that spot even though it was the best place to do pioneering work.

In forty-three years of Scouting, I can count on one hand the number of camping trips we packed up and went home because of some calamity. We never went home because of rain, or cold, or bugs. However, one such occasion occurred in December in the late 1980s, around 1989, I believe. There is no record of it in our official records, but it happened.

We went to the Fair Grounds in Statesboro on a cold weekend night. The Fair Grounds had no trees for shelter and we were given an area to set up that was as bald as a basketball. It was cold and getting colder. The wind from the north was at about ten to twenty miles per hour. It made the outside temperature feel colder than the 30-something degrees Fahrenheit that was predicted. That night the winds picked up and blew down all our tarps we had erected. Our troop was very proficient at setting up camp, especially in the dark. The tarps were erected over the kitchen boxes, ready for breakfast. However, the wind had other ideas and uprooted all the stakes and pulled everything down.

The temperature dropped to about five degrees Fahrenheit. It was a shock to come outside the tent into frigid cold, blowing air. We re-erected our tarps and began to cook. The youngest Scouts were having trouble. They could not get a fire hot enough to cook in cast iron skillets. I stepped in and helped them get a fire going on their gas stove and decided to help them cook so they could eat. Normally, I would let them struggle, but not today, not in frigid conditions. Meanwhile, the tarp blew down again. All the tarps blew down, the wind was sustained at over twenty miles per hour and it was all anyone could do to hold a pole upright.

While cooking pancakes, one of the youngest Scouts looked up at me and said, “Gosh Mr. Ken, you cook the best pancakes of anybody in the world!” Well, that was a great compliment, and it made me feel good that he still had a positive attitude, even though these were very tough conditions. They ate, put their tarp back up again and, as we cleaned up breakfast, the tarp blew down for the fourth time.

I looked at Donnie, Donnie looked at me, I said, “Donnie, this should be fun, but it’s not. This is torture and we are all freezing to death. How about we pack it up and go home?”

Donnie put it to a vote and every Scout said the same thing, we aren’t having fun and this is not teaching us anything. So, we packed up everything that

Saturday morning and headed for Rincon. Parents met us at the covered shelter where we sorted out equipment and everyone went home. I think Donnie and I got some extra kudos from the parents for having some common sense.

I was encouraged to write a book about our Scout Troop and its adventures. The problem is in half a century, we have attended over 400 events – that is camping, hiking, canoeing, tubing, and other adventures. That will be another story, but I think I need to mention a few more highlights up through 2005.

We have used Logs Landing Scout camp since 1977. There was an old building on the property donated by the Georgia Department of Transportation. The building had three rooms. A great Room about 12' by 20', then a small kitchen with water, gas stove, and refrigerator, and a bathroom with a porcelain seat and flushing water. A Scout leader's friend.

We had pancake eating contests at a picnic table outside the building. Inside, we were busy stacking up the pancakes and making sure syrup was on the table. We also held Cub Scout Day Camp in Effingham at Logs Landing, where we used the covered shelter, the building, and tarps set up as activity areas. During winter months, when we held district meetings, roundtables, and meetings with the Scout Executive, the building was a perfect meeting place.

In the 1980s we found out there was a property line dispute. Eventually, someone entered the old building and beat to pieces the toilet, the sink, the stove, knocked out all the wall switches, the wall outlets, and broke all the fixtures out of the ceiling, and finally broke out all the windows. The building was destroyed. Currently, the property line has a fence established by the current owner. The Sheriff's Office conducted the investigation, but we never heard back as to the outcome. We have learned to live with that situation.

Our troop put together two Paul Bunyan District Camporees, October 1979 and May of 1987. Both Camporee patches were designed by Donnie B. and myself. We hosted the event and provided judges for all the events (our troop did not compete). To keep the Camporee simple and doable, we had decided on ten events: knot tying, log rolling, crosscut saw wood slice, tree identification, first aid test, rope throw log raise and clove hitch tie off, match splitting, flint and steel fire starting, and patrol flag competition. In addition, we had a campsite inspection, based on a 1,000 point inspection sheet developed by Donnie and me.

In this Camporee, for each event there were clear winners. We gave out one blue, one red, and one yellow ribbon for each event. For the campsite inspection, there was only one winner, one second place and one third place ribbon. Competing in this camporee were eleven Scout troops from Effingham, Screven, and Chatham counties.

All of us were camped at Logs Landing, a small camping area of about twenty acres along Ebenezer Creek. Not far from this spot, about a mile or so eastward, is the monument to the old original city of Ebenezer. This area was full of malaria and disease, so they moved the city to the current location of Ebenezer on a bluff overlooking the Savannah River. This high spot on the bluff provided cool breezes and kept diseases to a minimum.

At night, for our campfire, we had the traditional Order of the Arrow tap-out for each troop. Order of the Arrow is Scouting's honor camper society where members are chosen from their peers. That night we had a ceremonial fire lit on the sandbar in Ebenezer Creek, near the old rope swing. Upstream the tap-out team put in a canoe and three members prepared to glide down the black colored creek water to the sandbar, and beach near the fire.

Two members paddled while the chief stood erect in the canoe. It was a beautiful, and memorable sight. Out of the darkness of night, on black water (colored dark from tannic acid from cypress tree roots), the canoe glided quietly towards the shore. The Indians stepped upon the beach and the ceremony began. From each troop, Scouts were called by name to receive the three taps from the Chief, and the Admonition phrase.

Later in the fall, an Ordeal would be held at summer camp to either put up or take down tents, clean up brush, rebuild broken walls, latrines, and repair whatever was damaged. Many projects were listed and each chosen Scout did these tasks as part of their ordeal with very little food and under a bond of silence. (Try to make any teenager remain quiet for more than thirty hours).

After spending a night out under the stars, with no tent, and by himself (out of sight of any other Scout), the candidate would receive his sash at the closing campfire. I received my Ordeal Sash at Camp Strachan.

Now, camp wasn't very large, I think about 90 to 100 acres. But, it had many winding trails, and followed along the Forest River. We used to camp at JC Point because it had four buildings with bunk beds and electricity.

One of the old tales that was passed down to all Scouts is that of the "blue lady."

According to the legend, there was an old lady with a blue light, I'm assuming it was a lantern. She walked along the far bank of the Forest River, or Burnside Island. Now, across the river was Camp Low, the Girl Scout Summer Camp. It was reported that Scouts exchanged flashlight signals across the river, but I never saw that happen. However, the boys were aware of the girls' camp across the river.

After our tap out ceremony, the Order of the Arrow (OA) Chief led all of us along a trail. As we traveled, the last Scout in line was stopped and put into a patch of undergrowth as his spot to spend the night. I was stopped at the edge of the African Village that was given to the Scouts after they filmed the TV movie series “Roots.” From my resting place, I could see the huts and thought about the show and how I was interested in the evolution of a people into fully becoming American Citizens.

I had my small flashlight I had hidden in my bedding and some bug juice I saturated all over my arms and neck and ears. I nestled down to rest, confident that gnats and mosquitoes would not attack me. I lay on my back and looked up into the heavens, and there he was. My gosh, a huge, fat, well-fed, raccoon was staring down at me. He was up in a tree probably ten feet above me, leaning over, staring down at me. I wondered if he was hungry enough to bite an ear or a foot.

Finally, I slipped off to slumber and rested until I was told to get up and take my gear to a meeting place. Here they took us out to a reflection point where we were to relax and think about different ways to help others, service to others, and brotherhood.

We began working on different projects around the camp to spruce it up, paint, rebuild, or other jobs. After our long work day, we were given a surprise meal and a ceremony where the Chief presented us our sashes.

When I think about how Donnie taught me about camporees and the OA I have to shake my head. He is a wealth of information and I have kept him engaged with the troop as an Eagle Scout point of contact. I’m proud of how we help the Scouts figure out the paper trail process. I am very fortunate to find excellent, dedicated, good men as Assistant Scoutmasters, Scout committee members, and parents. We have thrived as a Scout Troop.

During the 1990s, many changes occurred at the 165th Airlift Wing. The unit Security Police were training with local Savannah Police, as well as other local police units, in hostage negotiations and anti-terrorist operations. I decided to put together a weekend scenario that would test the unit's ability to secure a terrorist threat on base and provide a chance for hostage negotiations.

This gives me a chance to mention Lt. Col. Mike S. and the exercise evaluation team I had assisting me for many years. Experience and imagination will develop a well-planned exercise and its flawless execution. The plan was simple; secure and take hostage the entire operations wing of the second floor. This included the Command Post, Intelligence, Tactics, Operations Center, Mission Planning, and an aircraft.

The plan came together when eight terrorists quietly took the Intel Section and tied up the occupants, except the Senior NCO. Since the Command Post was next door we made the Intel NCO ask for permission to enter. When they clicked the buzzer to come in, we rushed inside and quickly captured the entire Command Post staff and all the major communications nodes used on and off base. This was so quick and violent that a pregnant NCO, whose name will remain absent, wet her pants.

Now I had a small tragedy on my hands. A real-life incident we handled immediately. She swore secrecy and we let her go and take care of things and go hang out somewhere else on base until the exercise ended. She excused herself and that situation was fixed. With all the command post people put into one room and all phones disconnected, and a guard at their door and one communications terrorist expert at the Command Post radios, we moved to Operations and Mission Planning.

Six terrorists rushed the ops area and mission planning rounding up all occupants and pushing them into the pilots' briefing room. One terrorist placed claymore mines facing all three entranceways to the Operations and Mission Planning area. This effectively cut off any doorway entrances into the operations area. I burst into a meeting room where they had just convened a board for choosing the next set of pilots for the unit.

The unit commander, the base commander, and almost all squadron and flight unit commanders were in this meeting. The Wing Commander, a former football star for Georgia Tech, looked up and me and said, "Damn it Luikart, NOT NOW!" Meaning, please do your stupid exercise somewhere else or at a different time. So, I immediately shot him in the leg with a squirt gun and said, "You're wounded, Colonel, and all you other commanders are now hostages. Get up and move to the pilots' briefing room and take the Commander with you."

The Wing Commander was so mad his face was red with rage. But, this was an exercise and they had to play along. We herded the bunch into the pilots' briefing room and put guards on them. We chose one young pilot, Jack, and placed him in the hallway facing the main door we figured the Security Forces would approach. We used duct tape to tape him to a chair with a few sticks of dynamite (fake, of course) to his chest. Next, we put our final stage of a plan into execution. Colonel S., and a terrorist member, walked down the back steps. After they left, we secured the last claymore facing that door.

Out the back door, they walked towards the flight line. They quickly crossed the red line, catching the eye of ramp security and made a dash to an aircraft with an open door. Once inside the aircraft, they secured the door, catching some crew members on the plane, they closed up the back end of the aircraft as well. In his briefcase, Mike had about 200 reams of paper with a message printed on them. The message read something like this, "This is a Cuban communist support group. We want one million dollars for all hostages; we want an aircrew, and this aircraft with enough fuel to fly to Cuba. If our demands are not met, we will begin executing hostages until they are fulfilled." It was something like that, I wish I had saved a copy of it.

With the top hatch open, Mike threw the 200 reams of paper out into the open where a gentle breeze blew them all over the flight line and base area where

Communications Flight, Supply, and Security Police buildings were located. Maintenance was housed in the other Wing of the hanger and those papers blew around there too. Now the base knew something had happened.

Phone calls were coming into the Command Post, but no one was answering the calls, unless it was a hostage negotiator. Security Police moved quickly to secure the three main areas affected, Operations, Command Post, and an aircraft. They initiated (exercise-wise) their checklists and all calls were made except what the Command Post was supposed to make. We had that area locked down.

It took a while, took some nudging, to get a hostage negotiator to make contact. The Security Police (SPs) noticed the claymore mines and the hostage with bombs on his chest. The aircraft was handled according to their Standard Operating Procedures (SOP). All seemed to be contained, but no hostage negotiator made contact with the terrorist leader, me.

While all this was happening, you could hear pages being made across the base. "Will Colonel so-and-so call his office," or something like, "Will Colonel so-and-so please report to the Command Post." Unfortunately, the Command Post was shut down, and we had all the Colonels.

With the scenario drawing out with no attempt at hostage negotiating, I had to force the issue. I chose the youngest pilot we had and had him go to the operations break room and yell out the window for help until someone on the ground finally answered him. I made him beg for someone to pay attention to the terrorist demands or we were going to execute the hostages one by one until they were met. Finally, the call came into the operations center that I was looking for. It was the hostage negotiator.

Things were moving at a snail's pace, but negotiations were taking place. The clock was now moving towards lunch, and to be honest, everyone had lunch on their mind, except for the Wing Commander, who had lunch and a meeting to conduct. So about an hour and half, maybe two hours into the exercise, the Colonel and the rest of the hostages rushed their captors. Quickly dispatching their guards, they started out the door of the pilots' briefing room when I yelled, "KA BOOM!" I had detonated the dynamite on the poor pilots' chest and we were all killed.

At this point, the aircraft was rushed and the aircrew on board overpowered the terrorists and the situation ended, tragically. Everyone was in agreement, however, at this point that lunch was more important. We set about picking up sheets of paper off the base, and cleaning up our claymore mines, duct tape and sticks of dynamite. The Command Post, Operations, and meeting room were returned unharmed, and the aircraft was opened up and checked and readied for afternoon missions.

I think the thing that stuck in everyone's mind was how easy it was to take the base nerve center and paralyze the base. With eight people and some imagination, we had shut down the unit. The fact we had every unit commander in one spot at one meeting was luck. That one event made the communications effort between the Security Police and other wing operating centers damaged. It did force the unit to actually open and staff, with vice commanders and substitute leadership. This they did from a second building, executing the base plan for such a contingency. A lot of lessons learned were gleaned from this exercise.

The fun part of this exercise was the fact that I had the base audiovisual unit film this exercise. Somewhere in the base archives, on "Beta" format, I guess, is this terrorist incident filmed from start to finish. That video would show exact times and exact exercise occurrences as they happened. I'm sure I embellished this story, but I think it's pretty accurate.

In 1999, an opening as Chief of Staff opened up in the 165th Airlift Wing. I interviewed and won the position and on January 1, 2000, I moved into the vacated Chief of Staff position. The name changed to Community Manager, why I don't know, one of those Air Force things trying to look more business-like than war-like. This move was about sixteen months prior to a very important Operational Readiness Inspection (ORI) scheduled for May of 2002. Six months earlier, the 165th Services Flight failed their ORI. Needless to say, there were many leadership changes in that unit the same time I came on board.

About this same time, we had a recap of the 1999 hurricane Floyd debacle. Georgia found out that the Hurricane Plan needed to be bolstered. It wasn't bad, it just needed to be fleshed out with more input from all the units in the Wing. In 2000, I was given the task to rewrite the Georgia Plan 500-1. I rewrote the Hurricane Supplement describing a *Hurricane* as Hyper War. In other words, everything is destroyed almost at the same time.

Just to get it down on paper, I broke the Hurricane Plan into three distinct phases. I want to lay them out for posterity.

Phase I: Pre Strike Operations: the evacuation of aircraft, vehicular traffic, preparing the unit for a hurricane strike.

Phase II: Hurricane Strike Operations: the unit falls back to Macon and reconstitutes.

Phase III: Post Strike Operations: Clearing the runway, mitigating damage, setting up a sustainable Field Operations or Bare Base reconstitution.

In essence, that was the framework the entire plan was designed around. I'm sure today's plan has been rewritten, but the same phases still exist no matter what form it's written in now. In writing this plan, I visited eleven different county Emergency Operations Centers and developed a list of strengths and weaknesses. I also visited numerous airports for airlift capability, and I explored bridges that may become damaged during a hurricane.

During this time, I also participated in War College classes at the 165th Airlift Wing at night. I wrote an article on fixing US Intelligence after learning of the intelligence weaknesses leading up to September 11, 2001. My paper, "Intelligence Support to Homeland Defense," was published in the Navy's "Center of Contemporary Conflict" dated December 2002. It was also published in the Air Force "Air and Space Power Journal," dated spring 2003.

Chapter 11

The Personal Challenge 2001–2005

Personal challenges are faced by everyone in life. A wise Scouter, Donnie B., told me one day that you cannot compare Eagle Scout projects, and Eagle Scouts. They are all different. Yes, they all follow the exact same guidelines and follow the Eagle Trail, the merit badges and work hours, but all projects are different. Thus, every man carries his own cross, but, since this is a snapshot of my life, here is a list of significant trials and tribulations.

I was busy, very busy, but every once in a while, I would stand up and look out the window. Nothing was happening, but I finally had an office with a view. I had spent twenty-five years in the Intel office. There were no windows in that office and it was tightly controlled, so, we had no wandering personnel just walk into the office. Unlike that place, this office had a view. It had large windows that went maybe ten feet high and about twenty feet long. It was an amazing amount of light. I had to stand up and look out.

The Colonel's office was in the next room. I didn't hear him enter my office from the outside, he just wandered in and saw me standing there staring out the window. "Luikart, what are looking at?" he said in a questioning command.

"Sir, I'm sorry, didn't hear you enter." There was a pause. "I'm just looking out the window, sir."

He grinned and Colonel W. said, "I understand Ken. If I was cooped up in a room with no windows, I probably would be staring at nothing too."

I was okay, he understood, and I tried very hard not to stand up and stare out the window and enjoy the view. Eventually, it grew on me and I totally accepted the light and view as normal. I had excellent help in the office, and they were able to carry out projects for me that accomplished interesting projects. I remember visiting several Naval ships that visited Savannah. Also, I was still a part of the Exercise Evaluation Team. A job I held since 1988.

As the year 2000 rolled around and our computers survived the change of the Y2K century change, new challenges at work crept into my life. Interestingly enough, I was tasked by the Commander to sit at my desk all night, with all the computers up and running (including the classified beast I had) to make sure the change of the New Year, 2000 didn't throw them off. Funny thing about that, we learned that the real new century didn't begin till 2001. So the next January, I got to babysit the computers in the intelligence section again to make sure they didn't crash. If they did, I had to start dialing numbers quickly, other than that, it was a dull night.

But later that year one of the leaders of our unit got a job as a liaison officer in the country of Georgia. He left his Director of Support position as well as the coinciding position as Commander of the Mission Support Flight leaving two vacancies. This job was important because the Support Flight kept all the records of people deploying on a new computer system that had just come onboard around 2000. It was called Manper B. It was complicated and difficult to input and it didn't work. Surprise, surprise, there were probably 1,000 major problems with the system. Each problem was painstakingly worked out over weeks and months. Meanwhile, we had a serious Operational Readiness Exercise to prepare for. It was coming, May 2002, just thirteen months away. I was chosen as the brand new Mission Support Flight Commander.

I moved into my office starting about April of 2001. I had experience as the Community Relations Officer, but now I was commanding a flight, and was the boss of about seven other squadrons and flights, including the Medical Group. The Security Forces Squadron (SFS) was one of my units. Every day I was receiving reports from Intel and the SFS about possible terrorist attacks. We already observed attacks on one of our ships, and the World Trade Center, and other places around the world. Tensions were high and the color of the terrorist attack threat was close to red, orange I think it was. (Something they don't use anymore)

We had some problems in the Mission Support Flight, we had a lot of new people in new positions. We needed to build and train a new deployment crew, fix our secure phone system, and get our Manper B system up and running.

March of 2001, I was cutting the grass in the back yard. I bent over to pick up a brick when suddenly my back gave out and I had severe lower back pain. It knocked me to the ground. I laid there for a while and finally, painfully, made my way to the house. The next week I walked around with my left foot exhibiting "drop foot." The foot would drag or wouldn't even pick up off the ground. It hurt and my back and nerves up and down my left leg were burning and hurting.

Finally, Sandi said, "Let's find a doctor that can diagnose and fix this problem." So off we went to see Doctor C. He was not old-old, but he was old. Immediately, he set me up for an MRI (Magnetic Resonance Imaging). I was to travel to St. Joseph's hospital for the MRI within three days of seeing Doctor C.

Here is where something funny, well maybe annoying, took place. It was Sandi's birthday when Sandi went with me for the MRI. I went into the imaging room and I told them I was a little dubious of being crammed into a noisy knocking machine. I honestly think two different people gave me a pill to take before I was scheduled to go into the machine.

They helped me into the machine, put the headphones on me and that's when I went blank. I had no memory of the knocking, or whatever they did, until they tried to wake me at the end. I didn't wake up well at all, I was rubbery. They helped me to the door, Sandi got the car door open, and they poured me into the car!

Sandi had to go find out some stuff for Jenny, and she drove by a building that was being demolished. All of a sudden, I started crying, "They tore down Walmart, look they tore it all down!" I wailed.

Sandi said, "No they didn't, that is an old building they are clearing out for a new one, that is not Walmart!" I continued to cry and sob.

Since it was Sandi's birthday, we decided to eat at Logan's on Abercorn Extension. I was still loopy, but I was upright and walking. I insisted that I was alright to go out and eat. We walked in and finally got to our table. I told the waitress, "It's her birthday." I grinned at her.

I think she thought I was creepy because I began to order everything on the menu. As she was writing it down, Sandi was saying, "No, no, he cannot eat that much food. Strike that; he can't eat all that."

As people squeezed by, I would stop them and say, "It's her birthday!' Some I told that to two or three times. Meanwhile, the waitress was getting annoyed so she left me and took Sandi's order. The meal was served and I was up and looking at anyone that would pay attention, "It's her birthday!" Poor Sandi was so embarrassed. She kept telling them I had just had an MRI and was still under the influence of drugs. I had been over medicated; I was only supposed to have been given one pill, not two.

After the monumental scene at Logan's we got into the car and headed to White Marsh Methodist Church for Sandi to go over the music for Jennifer's wedding. Jenny, being a music teacher, wanted special music and Sandi had found it. Sandi finally reached the church. She had an appointment to talk with the organist. Sandi asked the lady if she would meet outside by the car, at this point she didn't want to leave me alone. While Sandi was talking wedding music, I found the electric button that unlocked the car, then locked it back again.

This is what I constantly did while she was talking, bu bump, ba bump, bu bump, ba bump, bu bamp, ba bump, and on and on and on I kept doing this. Finally, the lady became annoyed. She looked at me scornfully, or pitifully, I cannot remember, but Sandi told her I was still loopy from drugs I had taken before an MRI. I kept doing it until Sandi got back in car, she said, "Why are you doing that? It's very annoying."

"I'm trying to get out," I shot back.

She told me to "Stop it, period."

So, I did.

With one last errand to run we arrived at the outlet mall, out by Highway 204 and I-95. There were many cool stores in this mall, one where Sandi needed to check out a pair of earrings for Jenny for her wedding. She pulled up right in front of the store, and was able to park in front of a large bank of glass windows. "I will be right back, you stay here, and be safe." She stepped out of the car and went inside the store. She wasn't to be gone but just a few minutes.

I was in a twilight mood, or zone. I was still feeling dizzy and disoriented, so I grabbed my GPS (Global Positioning System). It was a blue handheld GPS and was very capable of guiding me to my destination. However, I had no clue how to put the men's room into the GPS. I wandered through the parking lot, trying to follow the lines on the blue GPS. I came upon this car, that car, another car, a truck, a building, and all the while things are getting dim.

Sandi came out of the store and saw me in the middle of the parking lot holding this GPS. "What are you doing?" she questioned in an annoyed voice.

"I had to pee," I replied.

"What? Where were you going?"

As I got to the car I told her, "I'm not sure, but I thought the GPS said pee here so I did, I'm not sure where it was." So now I'm a possible felon in Georgia for pulling private parts out in public, but I had to go, and GPS said do it HERE! We have since figured out I did make it to the men's room.

That was a memorable birthday for Sandi, albeit, a really terrible one. I hardly remember it. I had to ask her details about that story and it's true, as best I can remember.

My dad and mom rarely came here to see us. When they did, strange things would happen, and I cannot explain it, but they did. One afternoon we all piled into the car and headed for a seafood restaurant in Savannah. I remember pulling up to the stop sign, I stopped, and fell asleep at our turn. *Instantly*. I was fully out of it. I had worked a long day, usually ten to twelve hours, in hot sun, and I was bushed. When I stopped I suddenly went into almost a coma, Dad punched me and said, "Son, you're clear to go now." That was all he said. I made the turn and that was the end of that.

Dad was a hoot. He was funny, and had a wry sense of humor. I see this genetic trait in myself, Dave, Dana, and all our children. I see it in my grandsons as well. Jamey's little boy, Nathan, my third grandson, while riding home in their car, out of the clear blue asked his dad for some money, "Dad I need money!"

"What for?" asked Jamey.

"I need to buy a house because I'm moving out."

Jamey was dumbfounded.

Alexander, my second born grandson, stood at attention and saluted for the Pledge of Allegiance. We were doing the flag ceremony for the veterans returning from Afghanistan. On the way home Alex quipped, "Pop Pop, that Pledge of Allegiance is way too long." He was unhappy standing for what seemed to him an eternity.

Roman, my first grandson, is so fast with his thoughts and thinking. When he was four, we were visiting Jamey in Florida. We were crossing the Courtney Campbell Causeway and he asked "Is that the ocean?"

We explained, "It's actually the Gulf of Mexico."

Whereupon he asked, "Is that where the chips come from?" He was referring to the chips we had eaten at the Mexican restaurant.

Another time we were in Lancaster County, Pennsylvania and had passed many Amish people driving buggies down the road. He even got to drive a team while we were in Bird in Hand. We passed by a covered bridge and he asked, "Pop Pop," as he pointed to the covered bridge. "Is that a car wash for the Amish buggies?"

I stopped for a second and said, "No Roman, that's really a bridge, called a covered bridge. They are found all over the place up here." He was satisfied.

So the ability to think and act and do is passed on from generation to generation. It's been in our blood for a long time. Luikarts go back to 1542 where we can find a birth record for Peter Luckhardt and his daddy's name was Hann. The Luikarts have been German for over 500 years. The desire to be neat and clean and keep things orderly is in our blood. I know I'm probably the least tidy Luikart, but my analysis skills are sharp. I'm not bragging. I always try to get it right.

My surgery for my back was done on September 8, 2001. They went into my L-5 and scraped bone and repaired a disk that was pinching the nerve going down to my foot. I went home on September 9, the day after surgery.

September 11 came and I was drugged up and in bed, laying quietly. I was up at dawn. The medication was making me a little shaky, I was taking oxycontin and the pain was subdued but so was my awareness. I was awake, and up taking my medication. I went back to bed and was watching TV when I first saw it. At 8:46, the first hijacked aircraft hit the North Tower. I couldn't believe it, I watched this with a bad back, on drugs, in bed. I was mortified at how they were going to save lives and put the fire out. After all, I had fire training in fighting a forest fire, but structure fires like this were almost impossible to fight. If the interior fire sprinkler system wasn't strong enough or even working, that was going to be a difficult fire to fight. I often wonder if the firefighters were looking at the steel structures to see if they were going to hold up because they had been heated under an intense aircraft fuel fire. This structure fire was burning at a higher temperature than normal. But that is hindsight, and second-guessing fire professionals.

Then, at 9:03, the second plane hit the South Tower. At this point, I was already on the phone to our Security Chief and I told him to get the Commander to close all gates except one and put out whatever necessary forces were needed to protect the base. Of course, he knew all this, and had already implemented my suggestions. We had an over watch that was back far enough to survive an explosive device in a car.

The base was locked down and roving security teams were inside and outside the wire. Unfortunately, for two Swedish students who follow C-130 Tail Numbers as a hobby, they were taking pictures of our planes through the fence. They were immediately arrested, interrogated, investigated, and let loose. They were told they would have to get permission from the commander to do what they had been doing. I don't know if they ever did or not, I wasn't part of that scenario. This was only the third day after my surgery and I couldn't go to work, even though I called Sandi at her job and asked her to take me to the base. She refused, knowing it was out of the question. I did what I could from home. I was out for six weeks, when I returned they had a big party for me, which made me feel great.

I was finally back in the Director of Support seat. I had a lot to fix and I was part of the Inspector General preparation team. I worked on making sure all checklists were current and were relevant. Also, I made sure that the team of Administrative Specialists was checking all Operational Instructions (OI's) and they were correct and relevant.

During this time, I attended the War College by seminar. I think there were thirteen of us in the classroom. We chose a seminar leader and began the grueling long study of war at the operational and strategic level of planning. I began writing my paper soon after starting the class on Transforming Homeland Security Indications and Warnings. My paper was much larger than the published versions. It was fifty-seven pages long with hundreds of notes.

Based on that monster term paper, I was asked if I would write an article for the Air Force Magazine and make a PowerPoint presentation. I gleaned 5,000 words for a written article in the spring of 2003 Air Force Space and Power Journal, and a presentation of my paper at the War College in May 2002.

From my presentation in May 2002 at the War College, a journalist rewrote my PowerPoint slides into a 2,000-word article for the Naval War College Center for Contemporary Conflict. The article is under Strategic Insight and is labeled "Homeland Security Intelligence Indications and Warnings." I was quite impressed he rewrote my presentation in 2,000 words, including a couple of pertinent graphs. In a way, I was honored because when the year 2003 ended, I had been published in two major magazines dealing with United States Strategic Intelligence.

Now, back down to earth. That and 25 cents will buy you a cup of coffee at a coffee counter. This will not impress anyone to promote you as an expert in the field. It will not get you promoted in the field of intelligence, or command, or serving your country on numerous deployments, wars, operations, and whatnot.

This was my bio written by the naval journalist.

By guest analyst Lt. Col Kenneth A. Luikart, USAF. Lieutenant Colonel Luikart is the air intelligence officer for the 165th Airlift Wing, Georgia Air National Guard. Colonel Luikart served 18 months in Vietnam; supported Operation TEAM SPIRIT in Korea; Operation BADGE TORCH in Thailand; Operations CORONET OAK and VOLANT OAK in Panama, providing intelligence support to anti-drug trafficking missions in Central and South America. He supported Operations PROVIDE PROMISE, JOINT ENDEAVOR, and JOINT FORGE, flying important airlift missions into Bosnia and Herzegovina. Colonel Luikart supported Operation SUPPORT HOPE, flying humanitarian missions into Rwanda and Zaire; and the 1996 Summer Olympic Games, where he supported the State Olympic Law Enforcement Command as the Senior Air Intelligence Liaison Officer for Task Force 165.

In addition, I supported Operation Enduring Freedom serving as the Liaison to the Omani Air Force. I supported as the back ground commander to the logistical support to the G-8 conference held at Jekyll Island and I was the point of contact for the 2005 BRACC base closing questions from Congress, and given the Major Command Inspector Generals "Coin" for maintaining a superior "Exercise Evaluation Team" (EET).

I received a superior rating for my Inspection folders, reports, feedback, and lessons learned. Of course, that won't get you promoted to Colonel.

So, after I recovered from my back surgery in 2001, I went back to work. It seemed like every section had a new computer system. Each system complimented another system. During any deployment the computer in the Mission Support Flight kept track of every soul on the base or those that left the base for any reason. That information had to be tied into the Support Flight computer that handed out beds and room keys. And all those systems had to be available and correct at the drop of a hat. I won't bore you with more details, but we needed a lot of practice making those two systems work.

As the ORI date approached at Gulf Port, Mississippi, I was asked if I would command a seventy-man unit across the airfield that was considered a bare base operation. We had a sprinkling of all the people needed to plan, and execute missions in support of the US Army or whomever asked for military airlift support,

My bed was a cot in a barracks with no air conditioning and the heat was between 90 to 98 degrees Fahrenheit every day. It was May in Gulfport, Mississippi. Since we were close to the Gulf of Mexico, the humidity was high and unbearable. The buildings were made of wood with no ventilation. I was lucky to have some smart medical help over there at the Forward Operating Base (FOB). They told me that eating bread and drinking water allowed the bread to absorb the water and that helps to pass the water to your gut. It would keep down dehydration.

I thought to myself, they are gonna think I'm crazy for doing this. I went to my cooks and I asked for bread on EACH table in all our operations. From maintenance to Intelligence to Aircrew Planning, I wanted a loaf of bread on each table. I had a mass meeting where I briefed everyone about our idea. When you hydrate during the day, eat one slice of bread. Do that all day when you drink water, and your chances of staying hydrated are enhanced.

In my office the temperature at floor level was 101F. If you stood up the temperature was 110F. You could hardly sit and work. Sometimes I laid on the floor to use the radios and phones I'd hidden under the table in case of an attack. I was wearing a flak vest that was heavy, and I had just had surgery seven months earlier. In a way, I was hurting but I stayed and did the job. On my first day at the FOB I worked an eighteen-hour day. I got four hours of sleep, to be awakened by fire ants biting me – inside my sleeping bag!

They had made their way up the legs of the cot and were attacking inside my bag. After shaking and stomping and spraying poison, I finally won the battle for a sleeping spot. Remaking my nest, I made my way to work and ate an MRE (Meals Ready to Eat) for breakfast. Eating a slice of bread, we began day two at about 0400 in the morning. Aircrews were breaking out the Air Tasking Order, (ATO) Security was going over their Rules of Engagement and all work centers were reading up on Nerve agent and Blister agent attacks. Yes, the people in the Air Force would be forced to wear their protective gear almost all the time on a base in a hostile area.

Well, the missions were flown and the base attack repulsed and our folks did good on the Nerve agent attacks. We did pretty okay until day three, with little to no sleep, we tried to implement a base denial order. Not an evacuation order or retreat order but base denial. That meant we had to destroy everything as we prepared to evacuate. Quite a feat, but my team of seventy older and more experienced men and women did an outstanding job.

All I can say is we did good on that ORI and wouldn't have another one until about 2007, a year before my retirement. How lucky could I be to be thrown into a second ORI? Shortly after we all slapped each other on the back, the second Gulf War began, Operation Iraqi Freedom. The Air Force had a unique way of mixing and matching units together using the specific number assigned to form a team of men and women. They can mix this team from many different units. So in a way, they can keep down operational burn out. One intelligence team from a unit in Baltimore can be paired up with the Command Intel team from Savannah. Very clever how that works.

In March 2003, the war with Iraq kicked off and soon became Operation Enduring Freedom. The Iraqis were defeated, and now we are supporting their nation in rebuilding and helping provide the police forces necessary to maintain law and order. National Guard soldiers and airmen are better suited for this because we belong to a Governor and we do many of the same things in the states. Water supply, Combat Engineers, mine clearing, public relations, and police are extremely important. During this operation we deployed almost 800 people in support of Operation Iraqi Freedom.

In August 2003, I was writing a scenario at Volk Field, Wisconsin. I was assigned up there for about a month, but I was called home to take the place of one or our navigators that was rotating home. He was the Operational Support Squadron (OSS) Commander and also served as the Liaison to the Omani Air Force.

I had big shoes to fill because he'd earned his Bronze Star over there during the war. Now it was peacetime, and time to cleanup and police the country of Iraq. We were in Oman, living there and working there, but flying into Iraq. I was a little behind the eight ball, but I traveled back to Georgia, got my chocolate uniforms (desert fatigues) done up with patches and badges, and I was manifested and ready to go.

Oman is where frankincense comes from. I felt at home in the desert. I did not know that every camel you see is owned. There really are no free range wild camels. The camels will only respond to their master's whistle.

Under their belly is the master's tattoo and you don't kill or mess with camels.

As the officer in charge of liaison every day with the Omani Commanders, I had to learn some of their manners and how to sit and behave. For instance, if you pick your leg up with the sole of your shoe pointing at someone it's an act of disrespect. They play the cat and mouse game every day to see what they can squeeze out of Uncle Sam.

Before I got there in August, 2003, the deployed multi-unit task force had an old wore out Humvee (High Mobility Multipurpose Wheeled Vehicle) and the unit let the Omanis have it for their Air to Ground training target for their fighter aircraft. The problem was the Humvee, it was taken apart, cleaned, received new parts, and new wheels, and was back on the road as part of their security fleet. Now no person in the Task Force wanted that to happen, but it did. So there was little horse trading after that.

Because I was the new guy a new request came to me to acquire a broken down wore out vehicle for target practice. I discussed this with our new commander and he was pretty adamant against helping them with any more wore out vehicles. I talked to the people in the vehicle maintenance shop and we came up with a plan that would make sure this vehicle was never used by the Omani government.

I went back to the Omani Operations Commander and told him he was getting an old bread truck as a target. His eyes lit up, oh, he was so happy. I bowed out and told vehicle maintenance to deliver the truck after they made modifications. They removed the engine, the tires and took a fork lift and drove the tines into the body making numerous puncture holes on both sides of the vehicle. The windows were shattered and the doors were bent. The puncture holes looked as though they were made by a 23mm anti aircraft gun. When it was delivered on the back of a flatbed, the Ops Officer had a fit. He told me that vehicle was unfit to be shot up by aircraft. I said, "No, actually, it's already a wreck but sturdy enough to last you several years.

Later they accused the US Air force of stealing copper wire that was coiled up along the road. This wasn't like little coils of copper, we are talking about coils of copper six feet in diameter. It would take a fork lift to pick it up and a flat bed to move it. I got with their Security Commander. I worked with cops at the 165th Airlift Wing, I knew I could work with this man. He visited me at my tent. Inside my tent, I had a black leather couch trimmed in gold (I swear this came from a house of ill repute) a TV set, a writing table, a table lamp and table, and a full size bed. I was a commander and this was a nice setup.

I invited him in and offered him tea and dates. He accepted, and we sat on the couch and discussed several issues he had. He said his men were not use to working with women as police or guards. I told him in our country they seem to do just fine and if they would look at our female soldiers as just a uniform with rank instead of sex they would be okay. He agreed and we moved on to women shooting on the rifle range. "Wouldn't women be dangerous handling a firearm? They might get the rifle jammed and kill someone unjamming it. They are not capable of handling firearms."

I reminded him that most of the women in the entire unit shot at least marksman and most security police women shot expert in the rifle, pistol, and M60 machine gun.

He got quiet, then we discussed the theft of copper wire. He asked if we took the wire. I said "No, we didn't and if we had, where would we hide that much copper on base unless we put it all in a building?" I was adamant with him, "We did not steal your copper."

Then I said to him "Commander, go to your local pawn shops. Check their invoices and check where they store metal. You will find your copper." We talked about that and, when he left, that is exactly what they did. Lo and behold, they found the flatbed truck of copper. An on base Omani contractor had taken the wire.

This brings me to the last bizarre thing that happened. Our airmen were getting bored so they bought some pretty high tech kites and put red green and blue lights on them. They were flying them at night and during the day in a huge open field. About 1600 (4:00pm) my executive officer received a phone call from the Omanis, "Who are flying spy planes on our base?"

My executive stammered. “Sir, as far as I know there are no spy planes in the air at this time.”

“Yes there is, I see it, I see it now, it has red and blue lights. What is it spying on? It must come land immediately or we will shoot it down.”

Well, my executive officer and I walked out to the edge of the field and there were three kites flying in the air. My executive officer called the Omani Ops Officer back, “Sir those are not spy planes, those are kites.”

“What is a kite, what kind of plane is it? It must land.”

The Executive tried to talk sense to him, “Sir it’s a toy, it has no engine, it just hovers up in the wind.”

“What keeps it up there if there is no engine? It is a spy plane and must come down!” “But Sir it’s just a toy?”

“A toy? Why do they have toys? There is no time for toys this is a military base all toys must be confiscated”

Shaking our heads, we walked out to the airmen who were having a blast. I explained to them that the Omanis thought they were spy planes and ordered them to be landed immediately. The men grumbled but were good sports and took their lights off the kites and gave them to me. The next day I took the kites to the Ops Commander and gave them to him, “How do these fly?” he demanded.

Well, I was at a loss of words, I said “Sir, it uses Bernoulli’s principle of high and low pressure, where low pressure is developed on the top of the kite and high pressure below it. That is what keeps it up.” Then I added, “It’s just a toy.”

I handed him all three kites, he looked at me and sheepishly said, "What do I do with these?"

I quickly quipped with Luikart attitude, "Take them home and give them to your kids, they'll get a kick out of them." He gave me a dismayed look, and I dismissed myself.

We had many talks about things in the Middle East. They like cats, they hate dogs. They kill dogs to keep them off the base, yet I saw maybe six cats running around the base. Those cats had very long legs. I swear the back legs were longer than the front legs. They looked like some sort of cat from outer space. I saw no dogs when I was over there.

The commander allowed me to set up an island tour service. The guards and I would take about six airmen out on a jaunt around the island. It took about two hours to drive. We stopped at some camel watering holes and a monument to the Indian Ocean. It was pretty neat. Halfway around the island we stopped to eat, guards always with us, we were unarmed, they were armed.

Eventually, a gun shooting competition took place. The competition was between the Omani Security Forces versus US Security Forces. Our women were going to go up against Oman's best weapons experts. This was a knock down drag out shooting match, and it had several parts to it. As I recollect the participants had to go forward with an unloaded weapon, hit the ground, roll into a firing prone position, lock and load, and shoot as many targets as possible in one minute. A target hit sounded a ping.

Later that day, it was a steeplechase across the open Omani desert to a flag that had to be retrieved and brought back. It was a timed event and the flags were probably a couple miles into the desert. The Omani desert where we were stationed had huge piles of rock a natural, occurrence in nature. Some of those rock piles were cobalt black, while some were cream colored and others were red. It was a fascinating landscape. I was anticipating and hoping that our women would do good, just to show the Omanis that their thinking about women was wrong. Women are strong, smart, capable, and can be killers.

So here is what happened. The Omanis have a great little gun (I wish I could think of its name), I think it was European. I got to shoot it and could easily hit targets. It used a red dot sighting system. So, the competition began and Omani jaws dropped as the women hit the ground hard, did the roll, loaded instantly, and fired. We could hear the targets sounding off, *ping ping ping ping ping*. Most scored very high in the competition. They thought the women were going to fumble around and drop stuff and get down like a lady should, but the US women showed them they were not to be messed with. After that day there was no more talk of women police not being qualified.

Now, for the other side of the coin. The race across the desert to get to the flags began. The Americans were trying to find north using a compass to orient their map. I almost had a heart attack, but they finally got squared away. I looked over at the five Omani teams, they were sleek, the maps were in their heads, and they were barefoot. I blinked, holy cow these guys were born in the desert, they were going to tear our butts up.

The gun was fired and ten teams, five American five Omani (I think it was five) took off into the evening desert. Each participant had to carry his or her rifle the whole way. The sand had cooled down to maybe 90F. I looked up, and ran up on a rock pile nearby for a better view. The Omanis were scalding our teams, our guys were slow and deliberate, but way behind. I sat down and waited till all ten teams returned. All five Omani teams were back, but the American teams were struggling. One team, then another, appeared on the horizon. As the Americans came running in you could tell the desert won, they were beat. So Oman won that race hands down. They are excellent shots, and in great physical condition.

After my ninety day tour ended in Oman, I returned home to find the next big challenge come my way. As soon as I arrived back in the US and had my several weeks of reorientation into the home, I returned to work. I couldn't believe what was taking place. The Air Force and National Guard were chipping away at our budget. As I recollect it was 35% of all money in the entire budget that was taken, and I had to sit down with my unit leaders to redistribute what was left. The next two years they combined to take an additional 16% of our budget. That hurt and it was unrealistic.

In June of 2004, I received two additional squadrons into the Mission Support Group. (the Army would call this a Battalion). A lot of command positions were changing and I had to honcho these changes as best I could. A worse problem raised its head, they were taking our trucks and sedans and giving us golf carts. We had, I believe, one Humvee on base, it belonged to Aerial Port. We had no deuce and half trucks, none. When the water got high in Savannah we had no vehicles that could traverse flooded areas. All I could do was argue and shake my head and watch assets disappear.

As 2004 and the war in Iraq was almost over, everything was shifting to Afghanistan. Bin Laden had escaped, and was in hiding. He would not be killed until May 2, 2011. The war dragged on and sometimes some of our assets would be deployed, but most were at home. This was the new world of mixing and matching Unit Type Codes (UTC's)

Because they wanted more money from the military for civilian programs, the Air Force was forced to down size to about eleven Wings and the US Army from eighteen divisions down to eleven divisions. As money was squeezed from our operating budget, conferences became almost extinct. Men and women you shared training with, attended ORI's with, and knew on a personal basis were kept from meeting with you.

Conferences were so squeezed they were one or two-day whirl wind affairs.

I wrote a synopsis of the war and intelligence in February, 2006. You, as the reader, can see for yourself if the Iraqi war ended as you expected, and is the war in Afghanistan going as planned?

CHAPTER 12

The Changes 2005–2010

I wrote this synopsis to Lt. Col. Lisa C., 146th Operational Support Flight Intel Officer. She used this in a book titled, *Networks, Terrorism & Global Insurgencies*. Here is what I sent her:

(Open Sources – Unclassified email February 2006)

"It's been a while since I dived into the Intelligence world, or even read a real classified daily Intelligence Summary. So what I have gleaned and came across is found in the current issues of the Air Force Times. What I've added is my perspective based on what I learned from the Vietnam war and fighting insurgents (Viet Cong and regular North Vietnamese armed forces.)

Recently a small squad of men, dressed in desert camouflage, blew up a revered Shiite Mosque. This was a surprise attack and devastated the Shiite Shrine, thus the perpetrators are trying to create a war between Sunni and Shiites in Iraq. What might be going on here?

Insurgents might be pulling their strategic vision from General Bo Nguyen Giap. General of the North Vietnamese Communist Armed Forces during the Vietnam War. General Giap stated that all insurgent victories begin with a "general vision." That is, you must have a creative application of military art. Secondly, any insurgent General, or leader, must have the ability to see conflict between himself and the enemy as "periods" of war. Having the ability to know when you have moved from one stage to the next in insurgent warfare is extremely important to success. (General Giap's book, Winning the War in Vietnam)

The war in Iraq is markedly different than Vietnam. Besides the vegetation and basic soil differences, the war in Iraq is a war of religious ideologies, versus a war in Vietnam between political ideologies. The war in Iraq is a war between different sects that have distinct differences in their religious beliefs. The result is the "Strategic Strategy of various insurgent leaders is faith-based."

Regardless of the political strategy, any insurgency will have to "keep the initiative" to survive. They will have to "outfight" collation forces, the(y) will have to outmaneuver us, and they will have to bring strategic destruction to specific targets = The Gold Dome Mosque destruction. By grasping the offensive insurgents can make the U.S. (and what they call the 'stooge' government) reactionary. It is apparent that the insurgents know the U.S. will not attack Iran or Syria. That they know that the U.S. is trying reducing the numbers of troops in country. Two very important strategic things to remember.

If the insurgents are smart they will make constant appraisals of their own capabilities. Their Army, its organic structure, the people of the country, and the country and its government (or lack there of) as well. They will look for limitations of Iraqi Army and look to fight the Iraqi's and U.S. forces in decisive battles. They must have the ability to change from a firefight to a decisive battle abruptly. We have seen evidence of this in the firefight in southwest Baghdad where elements of the 101st Abn Div were attacked numerous times in a simple meeting engagement.

The Vietnamese Communists broke their country down into three strategic – geographic areas. The highlands, the plains, and urban areas. You see some similarities in Iraqi insurgents in their make up. They have city and small village terrorist cells. These cells operate only in the vicinity of where they were recruited from. They also have, basically, three more 'nationalistic' terrorist groups. Ansar al Sunna; Secret Islamic Army; and Abu Ayman Network (an Iraqi Intelligence General runs this one). These more nationalistic insurgent groups have a Command and Control structure; sniper teams; improvised explosive teams; mortar teams; Intel/recon teams; and logistics support.

The logistics support would include procurement of explosives, small arms, ammo, transportation (vehicles), and establishment of safe houses. The Abu Ayman Network is known to have ties with Syria. They receive intelligence, and even manpower from Syria.

The insurgents in Iraq mirror, to some degree, the Vietnamese Communists force structure. A regular Army, Regional Forces, and Military Self Defense Forces. The insurgency in Iraq is in it's infant stage where the standing Army is still a "Regional" force, but one could conclude that perhaps adjacent countries provide the "standing" army. Regardless, the doctrine of the insurgents is urban warfare and suicide attacks.

In Afghanistan, the Command and Control is located in Pakistan, but the individual cell leaders are located in safe areas inside Afghanistan. Each cell has sub cells, and would be considered either 'regional' or local 'self-defense' forces.

Here is what's going on. First, a Regional Force, supported by numerous local self-defense forces, can do three things; they can move rapidly from area to area (city to city); they are capable of combining numerous smaller cells into a larger fighting regular force; they will target vital areas or towns. This distinctly mirrors the NVA/VC structure in Vietnam.

Secondly, insurgent forces are using the OODA Loop to their advantage. They are able to asses the situation, acquire intelligence on situations, adapt technologies, innovate their training, and market a new battlefield product quicker than we can. The enemy is, in estimation, out-thinking us at this juncture. Recently they came up with 'ground to air' improvised explosive devices. By studying helicopter logistic routes they invented mortars that spring up into the air and explode knocking down a helicopter. In addition, SA-7's are coming back into the region, which means they are getting some type of outside backing, or, they have been able to hide a good many of them from our troops.

The tough part about much of this is that many of the cells we face are small in nature. The Ohio group they just arrested was about 54 people. Small cells like this are found around the world, many in westernized urban areas. It makes it tough to crack these smaller 'localized' self-defense units. Tactical in nature, but capable of carrying out great strategic tragedy.

The Vietnamese bragged about their logistics tail. They had strategic roads, tactical roads, and were very smart in providing outstanding logistical support for every battle. In Vietnam, 'behind every battlefront was a logistical and technical base.' (General Giap) This logistics tail is also present in Iraq. Probably not well mapped, it does exist. On this strategic or tactical road map, they are capable of moving large numbers of people and material.

Having this "Regional" force structure, the Iraqis are capable (of) doing the following;

1. *Support continuous attacks*
2. *Attack police and army units in the country-side and towns*
3. *Wipe out garrisons*
4. *Shatter grassroots support for the Iraqi Army*
5. *Smash the Iraqi Army and demoralize it, make it fight each other (Thus the destruction of Shiite and Sunni Mosques in Iraq).*

One thought here (as it was with the NVA in Vietnam) was to cause agitation in the enemy soldier's ranks to bring about disintegration of the Iraqi National Army. Two, breaking up the 'puppet' coercive machine in city wards and districts, villages, and hamlets. To destroy the local and popular Iraqi Government.

Any good insurgent General would look at the Country as a whole, to find the area, or areas, to bring about a decisive blow to cause total disintegration of the enemy force...The destruction of the Gold Dome Mosque (as an example).

Any focus of insurgents is the capital city. Insurgents are already there. Thus, insurgents must find a way to handle the 'direction' of the war, or 'space factor' of warfare. They must be able to choose where to deliver the blows to U.S. and Iraqi Government. They must choose the right time to attack, and be able to handle the time factor of war. Mobility and concentration of forces is the key to their success. They will bring force on a spot of their choosing, and they will do this with highly mobile forces.

Vietnamese use a rule of thumb. They had a tendency to attack large forces in their rear areas. Thus, upsetting their 'battle array.' then they would encircle the enemy, split them, and then wipe them out. A tactic we saw used by the FARC in Colombia.

The bottom line here is insurgents in Iraq will attempt to lure the U.S. and Iraqi Government into making mistakes. The U.S. and Iraqi Government will suffer surprise. They will suffer surprise in the types of targets chosen. They will suffer surprise by the method of attacks. They will suffer from the timing of the attacks. They will suffer from the 'scale' of the attacks... (Nukes? Chemicals? Biological?)

Regardless, the insurgents will attempt to push forward the above agenda to run America home, like Vietnam. They feel we don't have the stomach to go the long haul. Remember, the UN has sat between Turkish and Greek forces in Cyprus since the 1960's. That's a very long time to remain in one country. Ultimately, they intend to defeat the "Government of Iraq, unfortunately, the sects hate each other so much, the result of that would be Hell on earth.

Something can be learned by knowing your history — Ken"

The history of the war in Iraq, the end result, and the war in Afghanistan, we are about to lose, only lends some credence to the assessment I was thinking about in 2006.

In 2005, our unit supported the 48th Mechanized Brigade's deployment to Iraq. We provided about fifty volunteers to help with the 48'ths deployment ceremony. Some younger people didn't understand the significance of this ceremony. When we deploy aircraft and crews and support people, we expect them all to return. Not so in the Army.

I predicted the Army Guard unit would take real casualties, deaths, during their deployment. Within weeks of their arrival in Iraq, they suffered twelve combat deaths. It was during this deployment that I embraced the Bible's 91st Psalm, the warrior's Psalm.

In addition, it was a terrible time to try to make ends meet in the military. But the real nemesis was raising its ugly head in 2005. The BRACC (The 2005 Base Realignment and Closure Commission) survey covered every corner of the base and numbers of equipment. A total of 17,000 questions had to be answered by every unit on the base. I was appointed as officer in charge of BRACC 2005, collecting and storing all 17,000 answers and had to be present when our commander officially sent them to congress.

In September 2005 I was told, along with several other Lieutenant Colonels (O-5) that Atlanta, or Headquarters, was refusing to allow the GS-14's to appear before the Colonel (O-6) boards. Even though a GS-14 is the civilian equivalent to a full bird colonel, we were refused the right to appear for the O-6 boards. We were not allowed to receive the "certificate of eligibility" that could be produced to show we had eligibility. I had completed all schools, and had worked through some tough scenarios as Director of Support. This move by the state meant for me that I was going to retire as a Lt Col O-5. It was, so to speak, the end of my career. Stinging from this rejection, I did not have time to lament and roll around in my own grief. A big Inspecting General Exercise (IGX) was coming in 2007.

I didn't have a whole lot of time to worry about my new status of forever being a Vice Commander. I had to worry about a paper war that was approaching. We just called it the "MEI" but the acronym stood for Mission Evaluation Inspection, or something like that. Inspectors from Air Mobility Command were coming down to look at all our operating procedures, and checklists.

Chapter 13

Life Springs Eternal – The Boys 2010

I know by now you are worn with all that I have done in my life. In the future, I can sit my grandchildren on my lap and say, as Patton once commented, "Grandpa, what did you do during the war?" I can honestly say, "Well, I didn't have to shovel sxxt in Louisiana." (Movie Patton, 1970) No, I didn't have to do that!

I grew older and wiser with stature. I helped a former soldier of the 101st Airborne Division, a man who went up Hamburger Hill, to get promoted. He was ONE day shy of being eligible for Chief Master Sergeant (E-9). There was a state policy letter forbidding his promotion, and they would not let him meet a Promotion Board because of it. I wrote a letter to the State of Georgia Adjutant General expressing my disgust for this state policy, reminding state HQ that policies are not really rules or regulations. It's a policy, and it could be wavered. The man was promoted.

These things do not happen just at the unit level, they happen at the Operations and Strategic level as well. An experienced Lieutenant Colonel pilot sitting on the ground in central Colombia had to make a decision. Prior to leaving the jungle, on that rocky airstrip, that was more vertical than horizontal; the local peasants brought a young boy to the Operations Center begging for a flight back to Bogotá, Colombia. He was severely burned and in serious pain. The local Ops Commander and the pilot made the decision to transport the young boy. Otherwise, the boy would have died. When the pilot let Panama know about it, they denied permission to fly the civilians.

The Colonel argued with Panama, requesting the argument be carried up the chain of command, since the Operations Major in the Panama Ops Center was denying the flight. After refusing to bump up the request to a higher authority, the pilot returned communications back to operations in Bogotá and the American Embassy, telling them he's bringing in a severely burned young boy.

The mother and the Colombian child climbed aboard a C130 for a flight back to Colombia. This was, for sure, their first airplane flight ever. When they arrived at Bogotá, a special team of medics and an ambulance was waiting to take the boy immediately to the hospital's burn unit. This action, this decision made by a local aircraft commander and his crew, saved a little boy that had been burned in the jungles of Colombia.

I wrote that colonel up for the Washington's Valley Forge Medal for heroism. His actions resulted in the saving of a young child's life. Here is the remarkable thing, and every commander knows this, those actions that save lives are not unusual. On the contrary, I know probably a dozen members of the Guard Wing I served with that saved lives. They saved lives locally and abroad. That is an American trait, perhaps a weakness, when we see a need, we are inclined to act upon it.

When I finally retired in 2008, I was truly tired of the military. I had served for thirty-nine years, with the exception of taking a one year break in service in 1974. By the time I retired, I may have been, not really sure, but I think I was the last member of our Wing that had served in Vietnam. I distinctly remember when the last World War II and Korean members retired from the Wing. Now it was my turn to bear the cross of being old.

My gosh, when I started with the US Army in 1968, we kept all records of everything pertaining to enemy units by pencil. We wrote it down on 3 x 5 inch or 5 x 8 inch cards that were filed alphanumerically. We used a large 8 x 11 inch card stock to write down information every day by pencil. When I retired in 2008, we had supercomputers that plotted electronically and kept data in data banks by electronic files.

In 1968, if you had to talk to another Intel analyst hundreds of miles away, it was done on a huge machine that was as big as a washing machine. When I retired, we had smartphones or BlackBerries. The technology boom was amazing, but I had no grandchildren. At an old age, you think you somehow missed the boat when you have no grandkids.

I was sixty, but still a kid at heart. My son and I opened a Comic Book and Game store, which failed three years later due to the bad economy. In those three years, I enjoyed learning about many card and board games. We had a section for miniature warfare games. We played a lot of Pokemon, and Magic and Star Wars miniature war games. It had been a safe, fun place for kids to play. However, the failing economy at the time left me with no choice but to close the store.

In 2011, my first grandson was born! He kind of just shot out, did a flip in midair and crashed on his back in a soft bed. Actually, that was a sign from heaven. This boy was going to become a smart, wise-cracking, young man. He was a fast learner. If he liked something, he knew all about it.

I had a Scout in the troop at that time that was the Chatty Cathy of our troop. No one could out talk this young man, except one little boy, my grandson. The troop was amazed, perhaps appalled, at Roman's ability to explain things in excruciating terms. His attention to detail equaled any British Colonel in the British Army. We watched him spend three hours explaining how to play games on the Play Station 4 (PS 4).

We taught Roman to use sign language before he could talk. Roman was signing, "I want more food" at dinner one night on a trip to West Virginia.

My sister-in-law, Terry, who was sitting across the table from us, said, "He wants more food, yes, he's asking for more food!" She could read sign language and Roman was making the sign for *more please.* He was just a little over one at the time. Later, on another trip to Pennsylvania, he learned to read at a very young age and ordered his own dinner when he was just five years old. He picked up the menu and read everything to the waitress.

She said, "What grade is he in?" The answer was he is in pre-kindergarten.

Roman is the oldest grandson now. He will always break new ground with reading and spelling, math, English, and whatnot systems that someone thinks up. Ever since he began school, he has read at several grade levels above his own grade. He is also at least one grade level, or more, ahead in some of his other subjects.

Alex, grandson number two, who came along in 2014, has his own personality. He was stubborn in coming along at the birth center, so, he ended up at the hospital where he finally emerged. Alex has his Daddy's looks, Roman favors my side of the family. Roman is left-handed and Alex is right-handed. However, both boys are ambidextrous. They are capable of doing some things right or left-handed.

Being number two is tough; it makes a tough little boy out of you. You're constantly fighting to get your own way, fighting to get the toy you want to play with and always coming in second to an older brother. I watched Alex kick Roman off of a slicky slide in a Florida park because he was there first. Roman was second, and he didn't want Roman standing behind him. So, with a swift foot kick, he forced Roman back to the ground.

Alex has a bit of temper. He smashed a television with the controller for not getting to watch the show he wanted. Yes, Alex is a little tougher in some ways. He will always get the hand me downs, and the clothes Roman had, But he takes up for Roman. Alex is more apt to stand up to a bully to protect his brother, and more apt to throw a punch that hurts! At the same time, he is a super sweet, sensitive child. He is very compassionate and tender-hearted towards animals.

At the tender age of three he once saw an armadillo hit by a car on the side of the road. There was a vulture pecking at the body, doing what vultures do. Showing great concern for the animal, he asked his daddy, "Daddy, is that bird helping that animal?"

Alexander is the grandson that helps me with the animals the most. Lucky, my calico cat, loves Alex. Those two curl up and lay on each other all afternoon. It has been this way ever since Alex was a baby and Lucky jumped the playpen to lie down and nap with Alex. I got a new cat from a friend that couldn't keep a cat at her home. The parents said she could move back in, but the cat had to go. Nala, a small gray cat, was untouchable when she arrived at my home. Once out of the crate, there was no putting her back in it. She was wild and scratched and hissed for about a week. I was surprised when Alex played for hours with Nala throwing a paper wad down the hall, the cat would retrieve it and bring it back to him, and he would throw it again. When Alex wasn't here, Nala would walk around with the paper wad in her mouth and cry.

Alex helps me with Cricket and Little Bit, our two Chihuahuas. He helps me feed them and he takes them for walks, and takes Cricket outside. He never complains and knows how to do these jobs well. I am amazed that the animals trust my grandsons. That's a beautiful trait to develop, a love of animals and learning how to care for them.

Alex is the grandson who loves to help around the house. He helps me outside when I'm working on outside projects.

Not too many years ago, in 2016, a third grandson was born. He looks like Amanda, our daughter-in-law's side of the family, but acts like Roman and Alexander. He likes many of the same books, and television shows, and games. When all three boys are together, they romp and play hard. I think what is remarkable is the way they get along. All three boys are very close. They have very few fights over toys, but when they do have a disagreement it's in a mannerly way. They play pretty well together, albeit noisy and rambunctious. I love watching them play, and think back when I was a little boy inventing our own games, or playing scenarios.

Their imagination and camaraderie impresses me and makes me proud to be their PopPop.

Nathan has his way of being direct, then following that up with a nice compliment. He spied Jennifer coming into the room with her summer dress. It had vertical and horizontal stripes on a white dress and Nathan piped up "Aunt Jenny I don't like those stripes. Go up stairs and change, but you are very pretty." That's Nathan, he doesn't hold back.

One evening, the Luikarts of Florida, were working at putting together a pizza for supper. Making it from scratch, the ingredients were strewn across the countertop. Amanda was busy adding ingredients and Jamey dutifully was trying to help. Nathan chimed in. "Daddy, let Mommy make the pizza. She's a good cook, but you're not a good cooker. But, Daddy you're a good eater!"

Although all three boys have their own distinctive look, when seen together, they look like brothers. All three boys have blonde hair and blue eyes.

I found out, not too long ago, Jennifer and husband Matt, are going to have their third child. It's a little premature to talk about a new baby in the family, but I am so excited and happy. I'm hoping for more grandchildren. I truly love those little boys. God has blessed me with. Everyone wants a little girl. We will find out shortly what gender the baby is and go from there. My bet is it's a boy. I just found out I was right!

CHAPTER 14

Epilogue

My greatest wish is to present all my grandchildren their Eagle Scout. I don't know how many more I will be blessed with, but at the moment, I will be ninety years old handing out an Eagle to Jennifer's new baby. I'm so proud of my grandkids, really, when you think of it all I am extremely proud of my kids and in-laws. All of us have worked hard to raise good kids, productive children that will benefit society.

As I stated before, what we leave as a legacy of our life are our children. If we leave children that are exposed to citizenship, duty to God, and an aspiration to help other people at all times, then we have left a real legacy. That takes work and dedication from parents.

I worry about my offspring as time marches on. I mainly worry about their growing up in this great experiment called the "United States of America." I am confident we have left them with the right tools to tackle tomorrow's problems. I pray that they will develop the ability to see fairness and justice, the love of God and

His commandments, the desire to help mankind, and to always do their best.

I have never been afraid to press on into areas that were new, or different from what I was used to. When I was a little boy, I always wanted to know what was over the hill, or the next hill, or the next. Usually I would find out by hiking over the hill unraveling the mystery hidden from me. Those feelings accompanied me to Home Engineering where every day was a different land survey. As a freshly graduated senior of the class of 1966 I loved that job because of the variety of experiences it gave me. When I went to work for the West Virginia Department of Agriculture that desire to explore gave me the will power to hunt down difficult oak trees in southern West Virginia.

In my years with the U.S. Army and the Air National Guard, I used those feelings to explore areas where normal Intel folks avoided. I would catch rides over to other air bases in Thailand to watch our unit drop paratroopers. I wasn't afraid or deterred by different languages or customs, I would press ahead. I have been to some pretty sketchy places in my lifetime. I have visited central and south Colombia, Peru, Bolivia, and other countries in Central and South America. Quito, Ecuador comes to mind. I remember the very large hill you circle prior to landing at Quito.

While in Ecuador, I was able to visit the equator and observe the experiments of water revolving one direction north of the equator and then going the opposite direction stepping just yards to the south of the equator.

What keeps us searching for the unknown? Wanting to find out what's on the other side of a mountain, or even explore the depths of massive caves? We are inherently curious beings. We are blessed by God to have a craving to seek out the unknown, to understand the world. It's why we get pummeled by questions from a toddler about everything in life.

Now I am in my last decade of life, if I am lucky. I look ahead and feel concerned for the future. I feel the same trepidation you get in your gut when visiting a new school house, or a new doctor's office for the first time. You lose a certain amount of curiosity when confronted with those types of unknowns. This year, 2020, has been the most unusual year of my life. The economy was bursting with gains, the New Year came around and 2020 looked so promising. Then a virus hit the world. A virus that rivaled the flu that struck in 1918. My grandfather survived that malady along with his brother Pearl. Now it was our turn to deal with a worldwide killer pandemic.

For three months, my wife and I held ourselves inside our house. Most all businesses were closed and those that remained open were soon picked over. Necessary goods became scarce, even fights over toilet paper ensued. Cleaning solvents, and wipes and sprays that killed viruses became difficult to find. My family remained at a distance from us. We visited Jennifer's boys through their living room windows. This was so strange to refrain from hugging and kissing your loved ones.

Now we are attempting to come out of this self-imposed recession, or depression, as some call it, and get the economy and life up and running. This is also a political year, and it goes without saying, every political year we have racial strife. It was that way in 1968, 1972, and so on. Four years ago it was waves of South Americans rushing our southern border. This year it was the result of police brutality in a northern state that set in motion another round of political turmoil during election year.

I can only surmise that this type of activity will continue for the foreseeable future. We are talking of having man on Mars by 2024, that's another political year. I would suspect any attempt at useful space exploration will be torpedoed by political upheaval. What can we teach our grandkids that will carry them forward into the unknown? How can we equip them to face the world's challenges?

Scouting will begin soon for all Scout Troops. We will have to follow a volume of new rules and regulations, as well as, increased costs that will drive membership fees through the roof. The Scoutmaster and their assistants will face challenges imposed upon them without pay. Volunteering to work with today's youth at no pay and high membership fees may destroy volunteerism.

A strong rooting into God's Word, the Bible, and Church will be their armor of God. Psalm 114 celebrates the occasion of the Israelites going out of Egypt. The earth and seas and rivers "trembled at the presence of the Lord, at the presence of the God of Jacob: which turned the rock into standing water, the flint into a fountain of waters" (Ps. 114; KJV).

Your children and children's children are your legacy. We live in dangerous and unpredictable times. The future is not clear; it is hidden behind the mountains of evil, deceit, lies, and the uneducated. The only way to see what's behind that hill is to go up and over it. To live it, to experience what lies ahead, good or bad. The tools you learn today, and carry with you tomorrow, may very well be the tools that provide you with success. I don't fear the future, I respect it, and I do not assume it's going to be easy.

Bibliography

1. *Roberts' Rules of Order* in 1876 (Wikipedia, 30 July, 2018).

www.ingramcontent.com/pod-product-compliance
Lightning Source LLC
LaVergne TN
LVHW041700060526
838201LV00043B/507
9781632215468